THE GREAT
Modern Pike Anglers

THE GREAT
Modern Pike Anglers

Barrie Rickards and Malcolm Bannister

THE CROWOOD PRESS

First published in 2006 by
The Crowood Press Ltd
Ramsbury, Marlborough
Wiltshire SN8 2HR

www.crowood.com

British Library Cataloguing-in-Publication Data
A catalogue record for this book is available from the British Library

ISBN 1 86126 876 9
EAN 978 1 86126 876 1

Frontispiece: The late, great Martin Gay with a fish of nearly 28lb.
Photo: Yvonne Gay.

Typeset and designed by
D & N Publishing
Lowesden Business Park, Hungerford, Berkshire.

Printed and bound in Great Britain by The Cromwell Press, Trowbridge.

CONTENTS

FOREWORD

Books on pike fishing tend to be divided into three categories: instructional, anecdotal and historical. I have always been happy reading any type of pike book, though the instructional stuff sometimes goes over my head (old age!). This book falls into the historical category and seeks to show how pike fishing progressed from the dark ages of the pre-1950s to today. Along the way, many, many individuals contributed to this steady evolution. I think it is to these people that the title is dedicated – *The Great Modern Pike Anglers*. Many take for granted the huge variety of pike waters we have today, the brilliant tackle we can buy and the bait in a bag available by just opening a freezer. Yet all this has come because someone else has thought about a problem and been bright enough to solve it. Though I wasn't busy solving problems in the sixties and seventies, I'm glad I was around then at least to see and experience first hand that time of change. A lot of us still go around muttering to ourselves, 'If I knew then what I know now I'd have caught a lot more'. The same goes for the tackle and bait. If I had then what I have now, it would have been so much easier.

Of course hindsight is a wonderful thing to have an abundance of. Unfortunately, no matter how much of it you have, you always find that the currency is non-negotiable. You cannot go back in time, and every day that passes is gone forever. That's why it has always paid dividends to live part of your life for the moment. Eddie Turner probably wishes he had patented some of the pike-fishing gear he invented or developed. He didn't, but it does not alter the fact that he came up with the original ideas. He can look back on that with some satisfaction. He probably wishes he had fished his chalk pit more, but he didn't. He did well though, didn't he?

We all have similar thoughts, and a cold day alone in a boat is when these thoughts wander along. What better way to avoid a touch of the melancholia than to sit and read a book such as this and realize that everyone in pike fishing has the same problems, even the most famous of the famous. Great new ideas and discoveries come along and everyone wishes he or she had thought of it years earlier! This book runs through virtually everything that makes our sport the demanding obsession that it is. If you are young or new to the sport then read this book and realize where everything has come from. A carp fishing-rod holdall has evolved unbelievably from a rolled up mackintosh! I kid you not. There are many examples like this. Barrie and Malcolm have given us all an enjoyable read and with hardly any instructions or rig diagrams!

Neville Fickling
January 2006

DEDICATION

We dedicate this book to Fred Buller, Bill Giles and Fred Taylor.

ACKNOWLEDGEMENTS

We are indebted to the many (living) anglers mentioned in this book who have kindly given us details of their pike-angling progress through the years, as well as numerous photographs and their opinions on various matters. The responsibility for any appraisal is ours alone, naturally.

Neville Fickling very sportingly agreed to write the Foreword for us, which meant he had a great deal of reading to do: we hope he enjoyed this, although we doubt if we could teach him very much!

Angling Times very kindly helped out with photographs of Derek Macdonald. We are also very grateful to Wendy Green who word-processed the manuscript.

We should also like to thank David Hall, Jim Baxter (*Sheffield Angling Telegraph*) and Ken Ball and the N.F.A. for permission to reproduce edited versions of articles originally published by them.

As this book went to press, we were immensely saddened to learn of the deaths of two of our great anglers, namely Dennis Pye and David Overy. We knew them well, and have to say that besides being real innovators they were lovely men, the kind of friends you need.

INTRODUCTION

Some years' ago we published a book entitled *The Ten Greatest Pike Anglers*. The number of ten was entirely fortuitous – we didn't plan it that way, but when researching the period from 1496 (Dame Juliana Berners) to the early 1950s (Charles Thurlow-Graig) we reached the conclusion that there had been only ten real innovators in almost five hundred years; on average, then, two per hundred years. These were, in order of their contributions (the years of principal written contributions are given in brackets): Robert Nobbes 1652–1706 (1682); Henry Cholmondeley Pennel 1819–1915 (1865); John Bickerdyke 1858–1933 (1888); Alfred Jardine 1828–1910 (1896); William Senior 1838–1920 (1900); J.W. Martin 1850–1916 (1907); Edward Spence 1860–1932 (1928); Sidney Spencer 1902–1977 (1936); Norman Hill 1903–1990 (1944); and Charles Thurlow-Craig 1901–1985 (1944). Their average age at death was eighty-one years which, given the time, suggests that pike angling is a healthy activity as not all these men, by any means, had a cushioned lifestyle.

We did not include Berners in this list because that work is clearly second-hand or, at least, indicates a very long period of (unrecorded) development. Similarly, Walton is least convincing on pike angling, in marked contrast to the remainder of *The Compleat Angler*. To many other writers pike fishing was merely an adjunct to salmon fishing or something to do when they were unable to game fish, and it shows in their writing.

If you look further at the above list, it is clear there is nothing recorded by way of major publication in the 1700s and it was not until the second half of the nineteenth century that innovation began to speed up: three major publications in the later 1800s, one right at the turn of the century, and five in the first half of the twentieth century. So things *were* speeding up and the earlier indication of an average of two per hundred years is just that – an average.

Table 1 is a summary of this vast earlier period of piking in terms of what was discovered and when. It is immediately obvious that a lot of what some of us have regarded as modern is, in reality, rooted in ancient times. But – and it is a big but – there really was a major revolution in pike-angling tactics and philosophy, beginning in the 1950s. The changes in the last half of the twentieth century far surpassed developments in the previous five hundred years and now places anglers in a position where *any* angler can be successful. Furthermore there has been a sea change in our understanding of the role of pike in the freshwater ecosystem. For the most part these have been changes for the better but in this work we shall not shirk from pointing out the downsides as we see them: that will come towards the end of the book.

Nor do the innovations of the twentieth-century revolution reflect badly on the old anglers. As the saying goes, we stand on the shoulders of giants. Robert Nobbes may have been the greatest, on whose shoulders all pike anglers stand, and in the 1950s there were those giants Thurlow-Craig, the Vincents, Denis Pye, Fred J. Taylor and Bill Giles. The debt of the moderns to these pioneers is huge.

OPPOSITE PAGE:
Table 1. Summary of major pike angling discoveries, who made them and when they were made. These underpin all modern pike angling and are discussed at appropriate points in the text.

INNOVATION IN PIKE ANGLING ~IN SUMMARY	pre-Berners	Berners	Walton	Nobbes	Pennell	Bickerdyke	Jardine	Senior	Martin	Spence	Spencer	Hill	Craig	MODERN PIKE ANGLING SCENE
Year of principle book	1496	1577	1682	1865	1888	1896	1900	1907	1928	1936	1944	1951		1950s---
herring deadbaits	?	→			?	?								to present
threaded trace		→												to present
static deadbaits	?	→												1950s to present
sunken float rig		→												1960s to present
attractor smells		→												1960s to present
wire traces, fixed leads									→					1950s to present
baked timber		→												to 1960s
dyed lines	?	→												1950s to present
ledgered baits	?	→												1950s to present
free-line rigs		→												1950s to present
eel deadbaits		anon 1957												1950s to present
spun deadbait			continued to 1950s											(especially 1980s)
legered livebaits	?													1950s to present
line clips														1980s to present
paternoster		?												
"walking baits"														
gorge fishing								ended in 1940s						1950s to present
trolling (≃ sink draw)														(in decline)
feeding patterns														1950s to present
"Bellars" hooks														1950s to present
half deadbaits														
artificials			?											
consecutive trace wires														1980s
growth rates														
Pennell tackle				→	to present									in decline
spinning flights				→	to present									in decline
spinning				→	to present									
outlawing of eye-socket hold				→										ended in 1900s finally
on-the-spot feeding														1950s to present
single strand wirekinks														
Gazette bung fishing														in decline today
sliding floats														
advanced paternoster rigs														widespread from 1970s
snap tackle with adjustable Ryder														
use of eels and smelt														widespread use in
use of artificials (spoons)		?	?											1980s
"shoaling" of pike														hot spot theory
Jardine snaptackle					to present day									
butt ring line floatant dispenser														re-invented by E.T. in 1980s
fly fishing for pike						sporadic to present day								
Taylor wobbled deadbaiting						sporadic to present day								
Trent Otter spinning flight														
twitched deadbaits														rare in 1970s & 1980s
mackerel deadbaits														
drifter rigs														perfected in 1980s
use of American techniques														
modern conservation principles														

9

By now you will have realized that personalities have been and still are important in pike angling. Whilst some denigrate any aspect of personality cults, we simply cannot do so in this book. Improvements in pike-angling techniques and philosophy, coupled with an increased understanding of ecosystems, did not happen by accident. It happened because some individuals had the drive, initiative and the questioning minds necessary to move things forward. For these reasons we shall try to give credit where it is due for the discoveries and advances, and we shall attempt brief pen portraits of the characters who dragged piking from, at times, a rather murky past into a rosier future.

Many of these anglers were way ahead of the commercial tackle trade and became professionals themselves, perhaps with innovative companies, some as guides, always as writers, often in the media of radio, TV, videos and DVDs. The tackle trade followed their inventions (for example, Eddie Turner's drifter systems) and made equipment widely and relatively cheaply available to all anglers. The same innovators made their techniques readily accessible through many articles and books, again benefiting the 'ordinary' or the new angler. And finally, out of this maelstrom of activity between 1950–2000, there came a new philosophy of pike and pike angling. At first this was embraced by pike anglers alone, but latterly has been recognized and adopted much more widely by diverse clubs and authorities.

Thus the Pike Society was spawned, then The Pike Anglers' Club; the Scottish Pike Angler's Association; an Irish version; a Dutch equivalent; a Lure Angler's Society and a Pike Fly Fishers Association. These bodies have influence to governmental level, in the Environment Agency, indeed anywhere where the aquatic ecosystem is being studied.

All this is a long story, but also an interesting story, and we shall now set it down for you to peruse and reflect on. There is a small number of warts, and these we shall not attempt to cover up, but for the greater part, it is a story of staggering changes and achievements.

1

THE LAST OF THE 'OLD SCHOOL'

The Vincents

Father and son, Jim and Edwin Vincent, were the epitome of Norfolk Broads pike fishing up to and including the 1950s. Primarily they used either elongate Norwich spoons – the Vincent spoon – or fished dead roach on the sink-and-draw or the troll. They did not use livebaits or static deadbaits or at least were not well known in this respect. Our old colleague Ray Webb knew Edwin Vincent and discussed with him the merits of the various methods. The Norfolk Broads was the Mecca for big pike in those days, and in the 1930s spinning, led by the Vincents on Hickling Broad and the Upper Thurne, went through a boom period. The techniques were little different from those used for a couple of centuries, though with gradually improved tackle from ancient times. Jim Vincent landed more than twenty pike over 20lb up to almost 30lb, and Edwin had similar results, though with fish up to 31lb.

We now know that, given that the location was the Norfolk Broads, these results are not all that spectacular. This is not to denigrate the catches of those pioneers, because they were amongst the first pikers to introduce sporting and sensible catch-and-release tactics, but it does reflect that the methods they used were less effective than the ones being introduced and refined in the 1950s. Edwin himself, in the introduction to Geoffrey Bucknall's classic book, *Big Pike*, (1965) writes, 'The present generation of pike fishermen has seen, and is still seeing, the greatest period of change that this branch of the sport has ever seen'. And you know, these techniques with the spoon still work well.

Dennis Pye

One of those changes was a result of the exploits of Dennis Pye (see, *The Way I Fish*, (1964)) who, fishing the same waters as the Vincents, landed vastly greater numbers of big pike. By 1963 he was reported as having landed 240 pike over 20lb and by 1964 he had caught four over 30lb. In one sense only was Dennis Pye still of the 'old school', and that was in using livebaits. Livebaits had been used for hundreds of years, so there was nothing new there. But not for him the standard *Fishing Gazette* (*FG*) bung and a small livebait fished 3ft below it and a string of small pilot floats. What Pye developed was the dumbbell float, two circular floats fixed at each end of a stem, and he fished moderate to large roach livebaits in shallow broads, adjacent to reed and weed beds and fished them in such a way that the bait worked the area and could be controlled in the way it did so. This technique presented a food item, which a normal pike could hardly resist, and the hook rig, a two treble-snap tackle (of Jardine type), gave reliable hooking. This method, the use of largish, lively baits, in swims where big pike were known to be, was clearly much more effective in getting the big ones than the techniques used by the Vincents. Later on in the book, when discussing the use of artificial baits, we shall return to this question because there is an anomaly hidden there, a puzzle that we shall need to explain. We shall return also to a consideration of Dennis Pye's natural successor, that most successful of Broads pike anglers, Derrick Amies.

Dennis Pye was controversial in one respect, in that quite a number of contemporary and later anglers disputed his catches. Successful

Dennis Pye with fish of 28lb 10oz and Derrick Amies with one of 21¼lb, Hornsey Mere, 1961.   Photo: Derrick Amies

anglers always have their catches doubted as jealous anglers seek to denigrate others rather than their own approach. But this criticism of Pye seemed to have more foundation than most. I met one angler who witnessed Dennis land a large pike and then return it quickly to the water without weighing it. Later he claimed it as a twenty-pounder. In the opinion of the observer it was not, and wasn't weighed anyway. This sort of story does nothing to help his reputation. In his book, *The Great Anglers*, John Bailey may have the answer to the conundrum. He points out that Pye was not interested in pike under 25lb, and may have rounded up some lesser fish to the 20lb mark. In fact, according to John, pike under 25lb were regarded as an irrelevancy. To anglers fishing lesser waters, away from the

Broads, such an approach may seem peculiar. And, of course, one must ask the question: if such fish were irrelevant, why produce a list of twenty-pounders? Why not publish, only, a list of fish over 25lb? The truth will never be known: Derrick Amies is convinced the Pye figures are correct, and he might be in a position to know more than some. Other very serious anglers, with records almost as good as Pye's, do have real doubts. But the *real* truth is that Dennis Pye was a master piker and very, very successful, with some principles of tackle and technique that need to be taken seriously by all pikers. There is just one area where we think he went a little awry, and that is on the subject of rods. The rod marketed as the Dennis Pye Pike Rod really was far too powerful, even for fish of 40lb

ABOVE: *Bosherston Lake in Pembrokeshire, subject of Clive Gammon's classic book* Hook, Line and Spinner. *Photo: Barrie Rickards*

RIGHT: *This is what has sustained pike angling through the centuries. A tail-walking pike on Lough Beg in Northern Ireland. Photo: George Higgins*

(which Pye never claimed). Rods have moved on really well since those days.

The Pye technique did not export well. This is because many waters in the UK are quite different to the Norfolk Broads in being narrow, smaller, deeper, lively rivers, Fen drains, giant lochs, and so on. But the use of lively livebaits was taken up by pike anglers, in conjunction with different techniques and this did, and does, produce good results. The Pye system does work more widely but it is rarely put to use. Firstly it helps if the right sort of water can be found. It helps to boat fish. And it helps to have a very good source of quality baits. Nowadays baits have to be caught on the waters being fished, on the same day as a rule, so that it seems unlikely that we shall see a resurrection of such an approach. We could imagine that, with a little modification, it could work well on the trout reservoirs. Assuming it was allowed, of course.

We do not want to give the impression that the last of the 'old school' operated only in the Broads, but it was the Mecca for really giant pike and did produce Hancock's record fish of 40lb (on the same day one of us – Barrie Rickards – had a 29lb 10oz fish in the Fens, only to see his 'glory' totally eclipsed in the press stories the following week!). In Ireland the standard method was the trolled copper spoon, a technique unchanged for centuries except that the rods and line were

better – the same cannot be said for reels and boats – and in Scotland trolling lures, often for salmon rather than pike, produced big pike at intervals. Livebaiting was also in use in both countries, and this was invariably the split-and-pegged *FG* bung, a spiral lead for weight (like the float, these leads frequently fell off!), and the bait shallower fished. None of these methods were new and, as we shall show, were not really going anywhere new, whether in techniques, practice, philosophy, or in understanding pike.

OPPOSITE PAGE: *The Montgomery Canal, where Thurlow-Craig did much of his pioneer work on early plug fishing in the UK. Photo: Barrie Rickards*

RIGHT: *The Late Vic Bellars, past President of P.A.C., superb negotiator on behalf of pike anglers. Photo: Vic Bellars*

ABOVE: *The pike in close up, showing head and gill-cover pores and, in this case, an unusually short upper jaw. Photo: Martin Gay and Yvonne Gay*

LEFT: *A pike scale enlarged showing growth rings and part of external layer of epidermis attached. Photo: Barrie Rickards*

Geoffrey Bucknall

We'd like to return now to Geoffrey Bucknall's classic book, *Big Pike*. This book captures both the ethos of the times we refer to in this chapter and has within it the thinking piker's attitude that will lead – *did* lead – to the discoveries that transformed pike angling. He mentions all the big captures, or claimed captures, of those years. But he also deals with ledger techniques on Kentish gravel pits, to which he used to gravitate in the cold winters (rather than fish the bleak Broads so much). He mentions piking elsewhere in the UK including, for example, Captain L.A.

Parker's success on the Hampshire Avon using a tackle rig designed for livebaiting in fast water: this avoids the problem in such conditions of the livebait spiralling to the surface because the tackle acted as a keel to the bait, keeping it down, and keeping it level. Again, this is new thinking creeping in to what had become a rather stagnant sport.

But something else was stirring down in the Norfolk Broads, which we have not so far mentioned. In brief, this was a man called Bill Giles, accompanied by Reg Sandys. They fished static deadbaits, hard on the bottom of Horsey Mere and elsewhere, and they caught big fish regularly. This was the very beginning of the new deadbaiting, which continues apace today, and it forms the subject of our next chapter.

2 DEADBAIT FISHING

It is almost impossible to overstate the importance and impact that deadbait fishing has had on pike angling. In the fifty years or so since it hit the headlines it is a method that has caught more big pike, for more anglers, than any other technique. It is used over a huge geographical range that nowadays includes Ireland, where tradition lasted longer than in most places.

It is important, too, to put deadbaiting into a full time context. Prior to the 1950s it seems hardly to have been used. True, in Berners' (1496) tome one can argue that deadbaits were fished on the bottom – and on Moreton's Leam in Fenland come to that – but the matter is not pursued, either by Berners or by later writers, except briefly by Pennell (1865). Edward Spence (1928) dismissed his own 'accidental' captures on deadbait as not normal behaviour. The reason is simple: in the 'old school' of piking it was considered that *movement* of the bait was the key. Therefore, lures and livebaits attracted pike whereas something static did not. The pike was not regarded as a scavenger. As we pointed out in *The Ten Greatest Pike Anglers* even the innovative Norman Hill seems totally to have missed the technique. In other countries in Europe the disbelief about static deadbaiting lasted longer than in the UK, so that when one of us (Barrie Rickards) produced the English version of *La Pêche et Ses Techniques*, French anglers totally refused to accept that pike would pick up a dead fish off the bottom – and that was in 1995.

Techniques in Static Deadbaiting

There was, therefore, enormous inbuilt resistance to the very idea of static deadbaiting, not least because lures and livebaits did work regularly and often. So how did it start? Who did it? And how did it catch on? These are enough questions to be going on with; we shall raise many more before this chapter is out. We have already hinted at stirrings in the undergrowth of Norfolk. We first came across what Bill Giles and Reg Sandys were up to when Ray Webb bumped into them on one of his forays in the Broads in the 1950s. In his usual very thorough way he had made preliminary visits to many Norfolk waters, surveying them, talking to anglers, carrying with him assiduously collected press cuttings about the Vincents, Pye and others, and when he arrived at Horsey Mere he found that livebait angling was not allowed and that the water demanded boat fishing. Not having his boat in tow he wandered round the shoreline just before dawn and found a swim carefully cut through a narrow channel in the reed beds. To improve access, some branches had been laid so that the angler could reach the water more easily. As he pondered this discovery in the faint light, an angler strode into view carrying a mountain of tackle. Bill Giles was the man and he proceeded to tell Ray what he was doing. This consisted of fishing four rods in a narrow swim, each baited with whole herrings. When he told Ray of his captures, backed up by photographs, Ray, metaphorically speaking, gave a great gulp! Back in Hull a week or two later, fishing with Barrie, he gave a detailed run-down of this – to us – totally new approach. It did not produce the results that Dennis Pye was getting, but it by far eclipsed our own efforts.

Deadbaiting on the Bottom

It was not entirely new, however, because within months it transpired that Fred J. Taylor and a

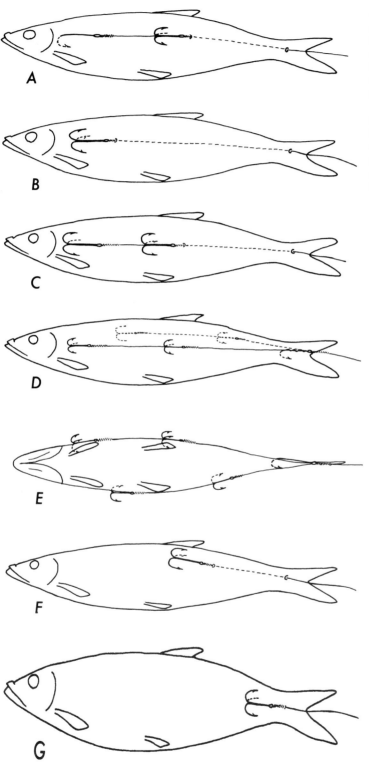

Evolution of deadbait rigs in the 1950s and early 1960s. The modern almost universal rig used today is a combination of F and G, that is, with two trebles set close to the rear of the deadbait. A, B, early simple hook rigs used by Barrie and Ray Webb in the 1950s; C, 'standard' Fred J. Taylor rig; D, E, Dave Steuart multihook rig using small trebles; F, one of the most successful of the early simple rigs, used almost exclusively by Ray Webb; G, a rig devised to beat those pike that mouthed the deadbait very quickly.

brother and cousin, were also catching double-figure pike on deadbaits on the bottom. Whilst Bill and Reg were deadbaiting because they didn't like livebaiting, and were not really into spoons, Fred J. had argued that since a lot of small fish would end up dead on the bottom of the lake by perfectly natural means then pike, in winter, when eels were dormant, would get used to them and could hardly be expected not to eat them. Fred and company used dead roach to begin with, but

found herrings somewhat easier to obtain, so he used them and found they worked well. Bill and Reg also used dead roach as well as herrings but eventually switched to the latter for the same reasons. Whispers of Fred and Co.'s successes at Wootton Underwood were on the grapevine by now, but the real publicity bombshell hit the angling world when their tactics appeared in a centre spread in the weekly newspaper, *Angling Times*. As we recall, Richard Walker was involved

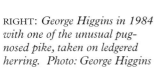

RIGHT: *George Higgins in 1984 with one of the unusual pug-nosed pike, taken on ledgered herring. Photo: George Higgins*

BELOW: *Half baits, one of the surprising discoveries of modern pike anglers, first spotted by Fred J. Taylor. The 'universal' snap tackle is shown in position. The tail treble should be slightly further back for deeper and more secure hooking, which also assists casting. Photo: Barrie Rickards*

in this publicity and he continued to write up the technique for some years, thus keeping the new idea on the boil and finally converting a generation of pike anglers.

Wobble Deadbaits

Bill Giles and Reg Sandys were, relatively speaking, of more retiring disposition and kept rather quiet about their fishing in Norfolk, although we were kept fully briefed by Ray Webb. There was only one real difference between the two approaches. The Taylor's used their deadbaits hanging head downwards, so that on retrieve they came back tail first. Giles and Sandys attached them the other way round so that on retrieve they could use them as wobble deadbaits! We now know that, ingenious though this latter approach is, it is based on a false premise: that the pike want to see a deadbait swimming head forwards! In fact, pike don't really care what the orientation is. However, there is yet another slant to this: Giles and Sandys had not quite shaken off the 'old school' ideas had they? You could argue that the Taylors really had rejected the past. If they wanted to wobble deadbaits then they'd do so in the 'normal' way but, when static deadbaiting, they'd fish them tail upwards!

Like most keen and reasonably well-read pike anglers we have attributed the early development of static deadbaiting for pike to Fred J. Taylor and Bill Giles – as we have done in several places in this book. Certainly they moved it forward. But we made quite a discovery whilst scanning copies of the magazine, *Fishing Gazette*. On 5 November 1936 R.H. Hudson described both static and suspended deadbait fishing for pike in an article entitled, 'A Fresh Herring for Pike'. He wrote another short article around the same time and there really is no doubt at all that this man was on to the techniques, and the rigs, long before our two famous names. Were they aware of his work, we wonder? We are very lucky to have a diary entry of Bill Giles dated 10 March 1951. It reads:

> The takes occurred at 12.30 and 2.00 [and] were had when spinning a dead roach. The first was a queer one. I cast, but before reeling in, had to clear

a tangle in the line. This accomplished, I recommenced winding, only to find that the pike had taken the dead roach while it was lying on the bottom.

From that experience they began to experiment, successfully, with dead roach, and then changed to herrings during a cold spell when they could not catch roach. All this was a long time before anyone else got on to the technique.

Hooking Methods

When it comes to hooking there is little to choose between the two techniques: the Taylor system resulted in the pike mouthing the bait more easily, because they usually swallow prey head first; whereas the Giles method results in less chance of deep hooking because of the slower pouching and the fact that the strike itself whips the hooks around from pointing down the pike's throat to pointing towards its mouth. Ray Webb and Barrie Rickards preferred the Taylor system and set about improving it by practical testing.

At this juncture we would argue that the Taylors, skilfully aided by Richard Walker, and Bill Giles and Reg Sandys, are amongst our first great modern pike anglers, because what they did formed the foundation of a piking revolution, which is still reverberating today and shows no signs whatsoever of a decline. That it really was so new, one can do no better than read the pike chapters in Richard Walker's *Stillwater Angling*, published in 1953. He doesn't mention the method and actually states that dead fish do not catch many pike. Fred J. Taylor in *Angling in Earnest* (1958), describes the new techniques in detail. So *that* decade was definitive.

The Taylors caught many double-figure pike, but not many really big fish. Giles on the other hand caught many pike over 20lb, latterly over 30lb. This simply reflects two things; the Broads are better – or were better – for pike than Bedfordshire; and in these days of the 1950s and 1960s big pike were not as numerous following the devastating winterkills of 1947 and 1963,

RIGHT: *Stanley McMullan does the honours for George Higgins with this 20lb pike from a stately home lake, 1987. Bait was mackerel deadbait. Photo: George Higgins*

BELOW: *George Higgins with the culprit of the previous photograph. Photo: George Higgins*

and, of course, fewer pike were allowed to grow up because most that were caught were killed.

One of the problems in early static deadbaiting was not the matter of getting runs, but of hitting the bites successfully. In addition, the objective of hooking the pike in the jaws (and not deep-

LEFT: *The essential camouflage of the pike.*
Photo: Barrie Rickards

BELOW: *Barrie Rickards with a Fenland pike of 29lb 10oz taken on suspended deadbait.*
Photo: Barrie Rickards

hooking them), proved problematical. Deep-hooked fish were quite frequent and led to the development of rather complicated unhooking systems involving very long disgorgers of a variety of designs. The opposite problem also occurred regularly, namely very large deadbaits, such as whole Norwegian herrings, being picked up by pike too small to really deal with them. Often the run was missed, or the fish fell off, or the fish dropped the bait before the angler could react.

Free-Lined Deadbaits

All these problems were compounded by what may now seem to be a rather odd factor: everyone free-lined the deadbaits. In other words, no leads or floats were used but the large bait was either cast, straining the rods of the day, such as the MK IV carp rod, or thrown by hand or throwing stick, allowed to sink, and the line near the reel set in an alarm or with a drop-off style indicator. If set up very carefully so that any twitch of the line was visible, this method isn't too bad, but in practice it led to far too many fish being deep-hooked. At that time trebles were large, always at least size 4 and often much bigger, so that unhooking could be very difficult indeed. And almost all anglers used gags, never a very efficient piece of equipment: Ray Webb was expert with one, but it still took him twice as long to unhook a fish as it did Barrie – more of this later.

Hook Rigs

And then there were the hook rigs themselves. Fred J. Taylor describes in *Angling in Earnest* that to begin with they had problems with the end tackle – the hook rigs. Eventually they opted for a tackle that looked similar to a snap tackle but with the trace threaded through the bait and the two fixed trebles towards the front of the bait, one just behind the head, the other one a little further back.

Bill Giles also used two trebles, quite large ones by modern standards and placed them part way along one flank of the deadbait. It was a similar decision, but without the threaded trace and, of course, his deadbait faced the other way so that the leading hook took a firm purchase in the head. Fred J. had to thread his trace to stop the hooks pulling out on the cast and to make the bait lie well, hooks downwards, on the bed of the lake or river.

Ray Webb and I went through similar gyrations to get a good rig. The problem with Fred J.'s rig was that it increased the risk of the pike swallowing the deadbait too quickly, and he is fully aware of this, as he makes clear in his book. Ray and I, quite independently, came to a similar conclusion, Ray preferring a single treble near the head (to facilitate unhooking if a pike did swallow the bait). His other rig had a single well forward and a treble halfway along one flank: again, in the event of deep hooking, this rig would be easier to remove than two trebles.

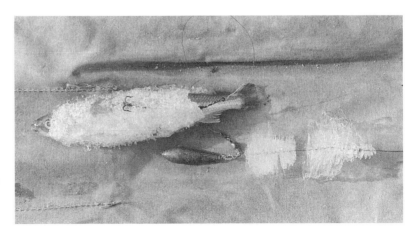

One problem with winter deadbait fishing is the weather! The ice on this tackle, caused by a frozen deadbait and water temperatures of 32°F, was enough to float the whole end-rig! Photo: Barrie Rickards

A finely marked pike but one with a divided pectoral fin, from natural growth, not damage. Such features enable pike anglers to trace the careers of individual pike easily. Photo: Barrie Rickards

Later Ray set the treble hook even further back on the bait.

I used all three techniques too, but I didn't like them, not least because threading traces is a fiddly business, and slow on a cold day. We often used to pre-prepare rigs for this very reason.

Anglers at the time hotly debated the whole business of deep hooking, and one of the major contributors to deadbaiting, Ron Clay of Sheffield, courted controversy by having the temerity to suggest that the best way to hook pike was in the top of the throat! Ron was never shy of being blunt, or controversial, and in a sense he had a point because hooks are quite easy to remove from such a position. However, the timing could never be guaranteed for this tactic and a second or two later and the hooks could be out of sight. Everybody abandoned this particular principle quickly, because something seriously better was needed.

Snap Rigs

Bill Keal's deadbait snap rig, described in Fred Buller's book *Pike* (pages 221–3), was a forerunner of Vic Bellar's rig, also claimed as an 'instant-strike rig'. Both of these rigs, with their upright singles, are no more instant strike than a standard Jardine snap tackle, which has, in effect, two upright doubles (that is, one point of each treble is in the bait, and the two points of each treble are upstanding). Nevertheless, it does show that anglers were trying to get their heads around the problem of deep hooking. Bill Keal, in his tragically short life, made an enthusiastic contribution to pike fishing of the day, not least by his superb photographs of the big pike he caught (*see*, for example, quite a few illustrations in *Pike*).

Hook Rigs with Four Trebles

One of the most serious and successful pikers of that time, Dave Steuart, came up with a tackle that he used very successfully on southern gravel pits and rivers, and a couple of his protégés, Peter Howse and Don Wheeler, brought the tackle up to the Fens where we gave it a thorough trial (and on Hornsea Mere in Yorkshire). This hook rig consisted of no less than four trebles, two down each flank, staggered, so that should a pike pick up the deadbait it would hardly fail to have at least one of the hooks in its mouth. An immediate strike was therefore possible.

Now, this was sensational news, because even Fred J. Taylor talked of letting a pike finish its first run when using trebles set nearer to the tail of the deadbait, and striking when the pike made its 'second run' was widely used by thousands of pikers, with deadly consequences for the pike. Dave Steuart, however, did something else that nobody had advocated previously, namely used small hooks, such as sizes 6 and 8 or even 10s. This was to allow the hooks to be set on the strike, which would have been difficult had the hooks (and barbs) been large.

There is no doubt that the Steuart rigs worked, and probably still do, but in our experience they had a problem or two, which at first puzzled us. We noticed that we didn't get as many runs when using this kind of hook rig! It should be remembered that everyone was still using free-lined herrings: only Ray and I of the anglers we knew, used floats – Ray fished the lift method with a peacock quill, and I used a tiny 'Pilot' float. What was probably happening was that pike were picking up the deadbait and were having difficulty putting jaw on to fish flesh! All they felt were hooks and hence

ejected the bait. Looking back this does, now, seem a little unconvincing even to our ears, but we did find that we got at least three times as many runs on the simpler rigs. Strange. Dave Steuart fished float rigs, we hasten to add, so that he could and did strike his runs as soon as he detected them. Malcolm Bannister (MB for short) has always used a float when deadbaiting or livebaiting. If you missed an initial take on free-lined rigs, using Stuart end-tackle you could have a nightmare unhooking problem. We rejected this system and it didn't seem to catch on widely, but as you will see Dave had hit on the most crucial issue of all, to whit the use of small hooks.

Barrie preparing balls of cereal and minced fish mix for deep freezing, as part of a pre-baiting programme. Photo: Barrie Rickards

Classic winter deadbaiting system on a bleak fenland drain, incorporating rods close to hand, comfort, warmth (note heater) and food. Photo: Barrie Rickards

Snap Tackles

At about this time one of us (BR) had been trying out snap tackles *à la* Dennis Pye, but tying his own from Alasticum wire and a swivel. These were vastly superior to shop-bought snap tackles because even in the 1960s these were too thick in the wire, and much too short being barely 6in long. Having tried two fixed trebles in the same manner as Fred J. Taylor and Richard Walker, he came to the conclusion that the fixed treble was not a good idea. Put simply, if one point only of the six available hit bone, then none of the other five could move and effect a purchase. On the other hand, if the upper treble was a slider, as in traditional Jardine snap tackles, then something could move and the chance of a purchase increased. Examination of the hook-ups in pike jaws showed that this is exactly what happened in practice. BR discussed this very question with that very successful pike angler, Bill Chillingsworth, who had independently come to the same

conclusion. Bill was primarily a livebait angler but when deadbaiting simply used his Jardine snaps, exactly as BR was beginning to do.

I think by now you will be getting the picture. Some very successful pike anglers, people who became quite well known, were all contributing, by discussions and practice to improve greatly a technique that was wonderfully successful even in its very basic mode. So we really had some great anglers involved: the Taylor's, Giles and Sandys, Webb, Steuart, Clay and, later, Bill Chillingsworth, all making small but crucial changes and forcing development of the initial, brilliant, Taylor and Giles discovery. I'm sure we are simplifying this just a little, because other anglers were around: but if they did not write articles or books or attend conferences and speak, then they would have kept us in the Berners' era. Word of mouth, in those days, took a very long time to have any effect and good ideas were probably lost before they spread and established. The writers,

ABOVE: *Barrie with a 26½-pounder taken at long range on half-herring deadbait. Photo: Barrie Rickards*

LEFT: *A well-formed winter pike on Barrie's preferred style of landing net with a 32in diameter round frame. The micromesh netting is not a good idea. Photo: Barrie Rickards*

Martin Gay winter deadbaiting on a small Fenland drain. Photo: Barrie Rickards

therefore, had a big part to play, even if they courted controversy as Clay and Walker did.

So what happened next? The clue is in the discovery by Dave Steuart that small hooks were more than capable of landing big pike. The big trebles were used in the days of billiard cue rods – very much overgunned in terms of both rods and treble hooks. It came as a surprise to learn that number 6 and 8 trebles, with their fine-wire construction could really bring pike to the bank. But they did, and they do. Barrie took up this small-hook principle having tried out Dave's multi-hook rigs and found that they really were the answer. Setting the hooks was easy. Unhooking pike was easy. And striking early was easy – with one proviso, which we shall return to shortly.

Summary of the Rig and Bite Technique

It is perhaps a good point to make a slight digression, to summarize the rig and bite detection technique now used by the authors and very wisely used by many pike anglers. The hook rigs do vary a little and quite a few anglers use semi-barbless hooks. Small barbs, even microbarbs, are really all that is necessary. But so many use what is, in effect, a sophisticated Jardine snap tackle using relatively small trebles. This trace might be 12in long and should be followed always, even in static deadbaiting, by an 18in upper trace. These have swivels and link swivels in the usual way. Some anglers prefer very fine seven-strand wire, but it does curl up badly after a couple of fish and we find PDQ or Alasticum or QED much better, in 20lb BS for most fishing. Malcolm uses 45lb Mason seven-strand wire for all his deadbaiting, no shorter than 18in long. The upper trace can be the same, but black, plastic-coated wire works very well. As we have argued, it is better if the upper treble on a snap tackle is more or less free moving, and more anglers are moving away from having this hook fixed – an idea that originated with Fred J. Taylor and Richard Walker. Malcom still has both his hooks fixed.

Distance Casting

Some anglers had tried using single hooks for deadbait fishing, even with large baits, and one of these was Vic Bellars, a past President of P.A.C. Vic Bellars first hit the headlines with a number of 30lb-plus fish (which he later thought to be one fish) from the Blue Lagoon, caught on tackle that he claimed to be instant pike rigs. That is, on getting a run, an instant strike was possible because the hooks in question were a tandem pair of proud-standing, back-to-back singles called (later) VB double hooks. These certainly worked for Vic but in our experiences elsewhere, and Colin Dyson's on the Broads using similar tactics, they do not work well enough, often enough. If you prefer singles to trebles then they are probably the best bet. But we did once watch Colin Dyson drop off several big Fenland pike using VB rigs. The main point is that Vic was trying something different, a new line of thinking. The specimen hunter Alan Beat devised a distance-casting rig for use with singles, further improving Vic's ideas. This rig is not dissimilar to the distance rigs used by sea anglers, but they have not generally caught on in piking in the UK. Vic may eventually be proved right, of course, to confound our current view. He has been fishing for eighty years after all! It is also worth noting about Vic that in the 1940s he was using a cycle rim as a net frame and a homemade net, rather than the gaff – he was before his time, certainly, but missed out on the 1950s and 1960s piking as a result of naval work and carp/tench fishing!

Lead Weights

Next is the question of lead weights. Nowadays everybody uses a variety of weight shapes and sizes – anything up to several ounces. The weights are attached by safe, breakaway systems either

ABOVE: *Mick Brown with his first twenty-pounder at 20¼lb, January 1972. Photo: Mick Brown*

BELOW: *Standard sliding float rig with, from the right: stop knot, bead with a diameter little greater than the line thickness, 'pilot' float, stop shot and, just visible, the swivel of the upper trace. Photo: Barrie Rickards*

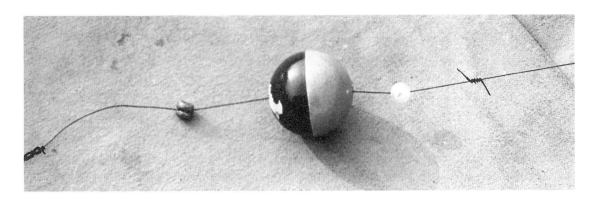

manufactured or simply by using a weak line connection (the so-called rotten bottom of sea anglers). The use of weights in this way is in complete contrast to the free-line systems used in the 1950s and early 1960s, ideas that stemmed from Richard Walker who argued that weight on the line meant an encumbrance and resistance. It does; but we now know that it doesn't matter. In fact, we would argue that in pike fishing (at least) the friction makes the pike move off with the bait. The leads we use ourselves are usually in the ½–3oz range depending upon the circumstances. The breakaway lead can be attached at the junction of the two traces, when it is considered that a short 'link' is needed, or it can be attached fixed or running to the top of the upper trace when a longer link is needed. For pop-up deadbaits it needs to be the former.

Floats

Then comes a difficult decision for many pikers: should they use a float or not? For us there is never any hesitation: we use a float whenever we can. The float needs to be slider and to be set just a little over the depth of the water to the lead. This is because a pick up of the bait, by the pike, will register immediately in some way, depending on the style of float. We suggest avoiding self-cocking floats, which really have no place in deadbaiting, as they mask early pick-up movement. We'll return to the matter of floats in the next chapter.

But what else? We always use a belt-and-braces approach if at all feasible, so we have a bite alarm and a drop-back indicator. This helps if you nod off or are otherwise inattentive – perhaps playing a fish on your other rod – and sometimes the drop-back indicator catches your eye more quickly that a float if, say, you are facing the sun.

We think you can see from all the foregoing that these systems, developed by the modern piker over a fifty-year period, really almost eliminate deep hooking if employed. Static deadbaiting has come that far.

The deadbaits now available and in use increased in the 1960s. Mackerel deadbaits were used in several areas independently discovered one might say. Thus Peter Wheat used them on the Hampshire Avon, Dave Steuart on various

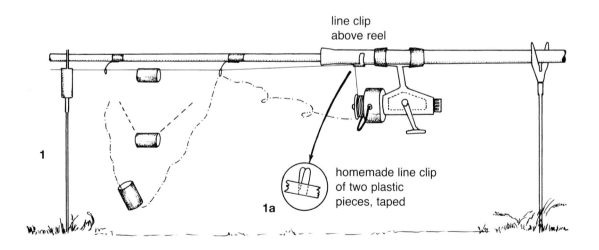

Belt-and-braces approach favoured by many serious pike anglers. It gives all possible chances of detecting a bite early especially if a surface float is in use too. The line is lightly clipped up. There is a drop-back indicator, which is easily removed from the line, and there is a bite alarm on the front rod rest. The drop-back indicator can, if preferred, be attached by a bar or cord to the rear rod rest.

southern waters, and in the Fenland an associate of the Northern Specimen Group began using them on the Great Ouse Relief Channel. This angler was a fishmonger and tried all manner of fish, but on mackerel he got good results. The problem everybody had with mackerel was that they were not only big, sometimes over 1lb in weight, but also stiff. The Steuart rig was best for them, but most of us didn't like this rig for the reasons we have given. And if the hooks were small, and you used only a snap tackle, what then? How and when did you strike?

Developing Techniques

As so often in definitive periods in angling, new discoveries of a slightly different nature came along at exactly the right moment. Basil Chilvers, of whom we shall hear more in the later section on lure fishing, had, for reasons of economy, begun to chop his deadbaits into two halves. Partly this was because he fished with his son and they shared out the weekend's bait, which they found rather costly. The results they had were so good that Barrie decided two things after discussion with Basil: one, the chopping of the mackerel and herring into two halves released a great deal more oil than merely pricking them, and two, a half bait goes on a snap tackle very neatly indeed and allows an immediate strike in full confidence. We now had all the answers, everything coming together into a very efficient system: quick striking; good, reliable hooking; good attraction of the bait; and early unhooking. When this was coupled with sensible modern float systems as described below, then a method of fishing was at last developed which has stood the test of time and is widely used today, not least by the present authors.

Bob Jackson and Mick Brown (with fish) on Ormsby Broad circa *1980. Photo: John Watson*

Types of Bait

Of course, not all baits were big. Sprats, for example, perhaps the most underrated bait of all, can be fished on a large single hook. Even so, snap tackles fish them perfectly successfully. It is of interest, too, that half baits were also discovered and popularized into independent quarters: one on the Relief Channel with Basil Chilvers; the other by Martin Gay fishing in Essex gravel pits. The Cambridgeshire Pike Anglers members had not at that time (early 1960s) met Martin, but when they did so a little later they realized that he'd got on to half baits and small hook rigs at exactly the same time as they had. And there's a twist to the tail of this story – in *Angling in Earnest*, published in 1958, Fred J. writes, '… If you haven't got a smaller one, [bait that is] don't worry, just cut the tail end off your big one and hook it on as before'. From the pens of great anglers…! He was five or six years ahead of the rest of us. Martin Gay, of course, we shall mention again and again through this book as one of the truly great contributors to piking.

A few other baits should be mentioned at this point. We think, although we are not sure, that Neville Fickling and some of his colleagues were responsible for popularizing eels as deadbaits. They are very, very effective baits, stay on the hook, are easy to cast, and do not get in the way of the hooks when striking. Just recently, pike anglers have stopped using them quite so much because the nation's eel stocks are under threat and, at the request of the national eel societies, pike anglers now usually buy their eel deadbaits from reputable suppliers. In the fens we tend to collect ours when drains are being dredged out, because little care is taken by the authorities to look after dredged out eels and it may just as well be anglers who take them as seagulls and cormorants.

The lamprey is another popular and highly useful bait, the effectiveness of which was only fully appreciated in the 1990s largely because of Neville Fickling's work. Barrie tried them in the 1960s, having caught pike with several lampreys in their throats. It was clear that they were feeding regularly on lampreys and that they would

make a good deadbait, but it proved very difficult to get hold of them in those days. The trout has always been a useful deadbait but may well be a little overrated – but see the next chapter. It is good to cast and stays on the hooks well, but our feeling is that other deadbaits produce more runs. Malcolm has found brown trout are good in the Lake District. There is still some scope for experimentation in deadbait species. Malcolm has caught on whiting. Few anglers have tried cod, haddock, plaice, flounder and so on. We have, but not with much success it has to be admitted, even after quite heavy and continuous groundbaiting. Anchovies are a different story. These are rarely used yet by pike anglers but now that larger ones are available they can be used as more than a mere additive to other baits.

Groundbaiting for Pike

There is a number of other deadbaiting issues with which we must deal. One of them is the practice of groundbaiting for pike (another Fred J. discovery incidentally) and the vexed question of pike that swallow the bait on the spot without giving indications of a run. You can imagine that the now-abandoned freelining method was problematical in this regard, and it is the reason why Ray Webb used the lift method: if a pike picked up his bait at all the peacock quill rose in the water and tilted over. However, those anglers who blamed prebaiting or groundbaiting as a cause of swallowing on the spot, were mistaken. Ray Webb and Barrie proved this conclusively by deadbaiting without groundbaiting on waters that had hardly ever been pike fished. They realized that if your bait dropped into a pike's lair (later defined for big pike associations as a hotspot) then it really had no need to run off with the bait: it simply wolfed it down, that being by far the most efficient way of avoiding competition for that morsel of food.

Prebaiting and groundbaiting for pike was really very slow to catch on, and even in the year 2005 is not very widely practised by pikers, except the more experienced ones, all of whom seem to do it, and to write about it. Fred J. Taylor may have been the first, but others were rapidly on his heels. Ray Webb and Barrie groundbaited and prebaited primarily with sprats, because they were cheaper. This was in the late 1950s. Bill Giles reckoned that his four-rod technique, putting out four herrings into the swim, was a good way to attract pike by smell – a form of groundbaiting. Barrie has now practised both pre- and groundbaiting every single year, on hundreds of trips, for fifty years and swears by its value. A whole variety of techniques have been used, including the following:

- Chopped up portions of the hookbait.
- Minced fish of various species either used fresh, or frozen into balls with a stone inside, and mixed with cereal as a binder.
- Putting chopped pieces inside a wire basket (the cormorant-avoiding method).
- Using fish oils in cereal groundbaits, again either solid or frozen.
- Carefully chopping up the remaining deadbait and prebaiting with it for the next trip.

As an aside we would say that those anglers who simply drop their used deadbaits in the margins at the end of the day's fishing are being wasteful and missing a trick. Why feed the seagulls? Many experienced anglers got on to groundbaiting in the early 1960s and it would probably be impossible to attribute its discovery, as a method, to anyone other than Fred J. Taylor in the 1950s. Neville Fickling did a great deal of work on prebaiting in the 1970s, and wrote extensively of his findings.

There is one aspect of prebaiting or groundbaiting however, that really has been understated. Let us take you back a little to the 1970s and 1980s. At this time it was fashionable to describe some waters as being herring-only waters, or mackerel-only waters. As a result pike anglers used only herrings or only mackerel. Not unnaturally pike were only caught on these baits! So the myth was perpetuated. And myth it is, in our experience, as is also the claim that pike will 'go off' a bait. This only happens when one bait only is in use, and there could be a number of reasons for the pike 'going off' the bait, including the possibility that the pike are not there any more, for these are hard-fished waters by and large.

If the groundbait used is varied greatly, a real mix of species and sizes of pieces, then our experience is that the pike never 'go off' anything. They may be feeding preferentially on mackerel one day and smelt the next, or they may have a day when they pick up anything in there. All this means is that the angler needs to try several baits on one day, and as multi-rod use is now the norm it is easy enough to do this. So few people have written in this vein that we reckon it was Barrie himself who put anglers on to this aspect of groundbaiting. It's commonsense and it is catching on, at last. It can't be bad for the pike, either, to have such a varied diet.

Small Irish pike for Barrie. Note cycle-rim landing net frame. Photo: Barrie Rickards

*Reg Sandys with a
25½-pound fish in 1964
on the Norfolk Broads.
Photo: Bill Giles*

We did not mean to imply, in the last section, that one deadbait is not perhaps better than another because, difficult though this is to prove, it may be so. Again, if we go back to Fred J. Taylor in *Angling in Earnest*, he said that his feeling was that the herring, a sea fish after all, was actually preferred by pike to dead roach and the like. We support this conclusion ourselves. Pike really do seem to prefer sea fish or other deadbaits to roach as a general rule.

The 1980s – Developments in Deadbaiting
Through the 1980s the range of deadbaits available to pikers increased considerably. Whilst one cannot generally attribute the discovery of a particular bait to a particular angler, one *can* do so in some instances. We have already mentioned early trials with mackerel – and we must emphasize here that back in the 1960s mackerel really did seem an alien bait to anglers, but the smelt was really discovered by Neville Fickling and popularized by him, after Harry Nelson put him on to the bait. And just think of the benefits that discovery has resulted in, for thousands of pikers. Incidentally,

Barrie 'missed' smelts as a bait. He tried them successfully, probably before most people, but couldn't locate them regularly enough, so abandoned his searches! What a mistake. Malcolm bought his by the 'stone' at Liverpool Fish Market.

Sardines as bait were discovered and popularized by Bill Chillingsworth, and they really did catch on fast. And they really could be one of the best baits ever. We are not suggesting that other anglers did not independently find out about all these baits, but they didn't write about them, report their catches on them, shout about them, or popularize them, hence one can only attribute discovery to those that did so, in these cases Neville Fickling and Bill Chillingsworth.

There came a time in the 1980s especially when many anglers tried many baits, sea- and freshwater, and it's probably impossible to give credit to those who discovered eel sections, or lampreys, or weavers, or red gurnard, or pollan, or trout, or bass, or pollack or anchovies, and so on. In part, anglers were searching for the magic, the ultimate bait, and in part they were recognizing, at last, that variety pays off. If we should have credited you with one of the above discoveries, or another one, please do let us know.

Colours and flavours and flashes are also aspects of deadbait fishing that are thoroughly modern, creeping in during the early 1990s for the most part. Many years ago, Colin Goodge, the Fenland maestro, came up with colour flashes, which he made of cut plastic strips. He gave some to Barrie back in the 1980s. Colin began by putting those bright red flashers on his livebait traces, and later put them on his deadbaits too. He noticed that baits so adorned did seem to get more takes; and it has long been recognized by lure fishermen that red flashes attract predators, pike being no exception.

Similarly, anglers began to dye their deadbaits different colours, or to smear them with an oily colouring. It is difficult to prove how effective this really is but it is along the same lines of variety of approach that we outlined above, and red coloration must attract on occasions especially if the food smells good. Malcolm's personal best of 33lb 4oz was caught on a yellow bait. But the argument used by some pikers, that a new colour gets around pike that have 'gone off' a bait, we don't buy for reasons already stated. Pike should not 'go off' baits if the fishing is done properly. Barrie has fished one private water for twenty-seven years and the pike will still take any deadbait even though they have different preferences from day to day.

Pop-up Baits

Another feature of static deadbaiting is the use of pop-up baits, that is the use of a buoyant material to lift the bait off the bottom. It could be argued that one could achieve this by use of a float, and simply suspend the deadbait above the bottom at the exact depth preferred. This also works, of course, but if the bait is to be fished static then a paternoster rig must be used, otherwise the tackle will drift away from the preferred spot. There is something about the pop-up technique, however, that makes it a bit special. The way we look at it is this: the pike is creeping about the bottom and to pop-up a bait so that it stands on its tail, just touching the

bottom, not only makes it slightly more visible but enables any leaking smells to stay down where the pike are. The tackle itself is less obtrusive, will not be seen by the pike, and will make it easier for the pike to engulf the bait.

As far as we are aware pop-ups were first used by Barrie and colleagues round about 1960. We used balsa rods, which we inserted into the deadbait's jaws, and we tried polystyrene chunks too. The method worked extremely well and Barrie has continued to use the technique until the present time. Now, however, one can buy pop-ups, red, round balls, which work extremely well and have the red attractor colour built in. Some anglers who have developed these, such as Mick Brown, have quite a sophisticated way of pulling the pop-up balls flush against the cut end of the deadbait by threading the pop-up line link through part of the deadbait. To Barrie this seems a bit fiddly so he simply ties the pop-up attachment nylon to a treble and lets them float free near the cut end of the bait. The only downside to pop-ups is that the pike do have to struggle a little harder to mouth the bait compared with picking up a bait lying on the bottom. After all they are probably much more used to doing the latter. The method used by Mick Brown makes it easier for the pike to mouth the bait than does the method used by Barrie.

So far we have talked only about static deadbaiting, and most certainly it is this technique that is most widely used by pike anglers. Even as long ago as the late 1950s, however, we began using suspended deadbaits as outlined above. One thing soon became clear, which was that it could be a killing method, either fished on the drift or anchored in position. The technique was discussed by Rickards and Webb in *Fishing for Big Pike*, largely because it was an under-used method and one surrounded by ignorance. For example, it was common to read that a good wave on the water increased the effectiveness of the deadbait because it gave it movement. We have two comments to make about that:

It imparts hardly any movement to the bait unless the latter is up in the waves themselves, and

It doesn't matter anyway because the pike know full well that the fish is dead.

This last reason struck some anglers as being unprovable. Not so. If you fish suspended live-baits and suspended deadbaits side by side, week after week, and the pike selectively take *either* the dead *or* the live, then that proves they know which is which, and they select according to their mood. The bait, by the way, does not have to be 'fixed' in a horizontal position, as we first thought, but can just be hung head down, or even used as a half bait. This may vary from day to day, of course, as all deadbaiting factors do, but it works as often as any other method.

So you can see that in the fifty years or more that static deadbaiting has been used, the originally pioneering techniques have been considerably improved in almost all facets, by experienced anglers trying out everything under the sun, often quite objectively, fishing one technique against another for several years at least. This becomes an important factor in the next chapter, so we shall leave it at that for the moment.

Methods Used in Deadbaiting

There remains one facet of static deadbaiting that must be dealt with before moving on to the next chapter, and that is the question of whether one leaves a bait totally static, or whether one 'twitches' it, or recasts it. And what is the difference between a moving deadbait and a lure or a livebait?

We need to go back briefly to pre-deadbaiting days. The reason Norman Hill missed static dead-baiting is because he, and all other anglers of the day, expected that only moving baits would succeed. Wobbled deadbaits had, of course, been in use for hundreds of years, and there is a strange, theoretical problem with their use if you accept our earlier conclusions that pike are fully aware that a suspended deadbait *is* dead. If that is correct then surely they know that a wobbled dead-bait is *also* dead. So it's movement that matters, not whether it is dead or alive.

That digression over, we can now return to the question of twitching deadbaits. Although static deadbaiting was well established and very widely used by the early 1960s, as we have explained, twitched deadbaiting came in very quickly. We recall writing by Jim Gibbinson on this; and most of us at the time tried one rod on the twitch on most trips. The technique simply involves moving the bait a few inches by drawing gently with the rod. Quite often this will be followed by an immediate take, as though the pike were sitting there watching the static deadbait. On yet other occasions they will not move to a twitched bait at all and require it to be left absolutely still on the bottom, often for many hours.

You don't need to be a wizard to realize that increasing the frequency and speed of twitching leads to wobbled deadbaiting eventually. And now we are back full circle because this is exactly what Bill Giles was doing, as we explained earlier. If you are using heavy leads the twitch not only moves the bait itself, but creates a puff of 'dust'. This in itself may well be attractive to the predator.

The subject of twitched deadbaits cannot really be credited to any one individual, because everyone of experience was doing it, and continued to do it until the present day. In a recent article Mick Brown explained that he regularly employed twitching of his deadbaits, which certainly confirms, if nothing else does, that it is a thoroughly modern technique. Malcolm often slowly sink and draws his deadbait as he reels in to recast or change his bait, and picks up the odd bonus pike. He has done this for over twenty-five years. This is also the technique advocated by Bill Giles.

If you *spin* deadbaits, that is retrieve them relatively quickly perhaps using a spinning vane, then the technique really comes under the heading of spinning or lure fishing, which we deal with in Chapter 4. But you can see how one technique actually merges into another: static deadbaiting (new) into wobbled deadbaiting (ancient); and both the foregoing combining into spun deadbaits (also an ancient art). It is time now to consider the modern all-systems approach to pike angling.

3 THE ORIGINS OF HOLISTIC PIKING

One of the strange results of pike anglers' obsessions with deadbaiting in the 1960s was that the very success encouraged anglers to have another look at more traditional methods such as livebaiting. This chapter is not wholly about livebaiting although we shall deal with that initially, but rather is about the holistic approach to piking, which really grew out of specimen hunting techniques, and which themselves developed initially with respect to deadbaiting. Lure fishing we shall only briefly mention, even though it is crucial to an holistic approach, because we consider that subject in some depth in the next chapter.

Techniques in Livebaiting

Livebaiting is a major part of the holistic piking approach, as we make clear in this chapter. It is controversial to some. One could argue that because there are two viewpoints on this issue, with perhaps a majority of pikers in favour of the method, then the method should stay as it is – with all the improvements outlined in this book now in place. That is the view taken by government ministers (2005) and by all official angling bodies. The best account of the status of livebaiting in angling is that given by Graham Marsden in 1993 (*Coarse Fisherman*). Vic Bellars, ex-P.A.C. President, successful pike angler, has not only argued forcibly in favour of livebaiting for those who wish to do so, but has equally forcibly argued for unity in angling on this issue. We shall return to unity as a subject in its own right in the Epilogue to this book. Here we just wish to say that such a senior and experienced piker, eighty-four when we wrote this, has seen it all and we

really ought to listen. Vic also points out that pike anglers, indeed all anglers, would be better protected if we joined the Field Sports Society (now the Countryside Alliance), but here again we see angling discord and disunity.

The 1950s

Let's begin by considering livebaiting, as it was available to pikers in the early 1950s. Most anglers used the *FG* bung as a float, and the bait would be set about 3ft below it, on a short wire trace of thick proportions and a length of around 6in. A lead, usually a spiral lead, was wrapped on the line and pressed in position to keep the bait down and to cock the very large float. The *FG* float was pear-shaped, fished point downwards, and was fixed on the line by a peg, which pushed into a lengthwise slit. Sometimes one or more so-called pilot floats were fixed to the (floating) line above the main float, their purpose being to give the direction of movement of the taking pike, once the main float had submerged on the take, and also to help to keep the reel line afloat. The *FG* float was rarely set deeper than 3ft because it was difficult to cast the tackle with the short, stiff rods ('billiard cues') used at that time. It also follows that distance fishing was out of the question. But distance fishing had become popular with deadbaiters, and that is certainly one of the reasons why the traditional *FG* system became questioned.

The *FG* system is, to some extent at least, unfairly criticized, because its design was of the time. Lines tended to be relatively thick, cotton, flax or silk, so that the peg usually did fix the float to the line. When monofil came in it was found that the floats were frequently lost! In fact, one of the design features of the *FG* float was that if a pike went deep into weeds then the float *would*

Roy Smyth with a 21½lb fish taken on trolled perch. Photo: George Higgins

Kay Steuart, seen here in 1951 with a 14½-pounder. Note the gaff, often used in those days, and, in the cases of Kay and Dave, properly used. Photo: Dave Steuart

Kay Steuart with a 21lb fish. Photo: Dave Steuart

come off and hence not hinder the fight. Similarly, pilot floats prevented the line sinking above the float: if that happens the livebait could swim up and over the reel line, which would lead to disaster if a pike took the bait at that time. (You still see anglers making this mistake today when it should be quite unnecessary). The spiral lead, too, did stay more firmly on a thick cotton line than it ever did on monofil, and it was easy to add or remove.

It is possible that amongst expert anglers of the day other livebaiting techniques were used, as for example, have been outlined by Bickerdyke and Hill: paternostered livebaits, and float paternostered livebaits, but one never saw these used

in the 1950s, only the *FG* bung system. The main drawback to the last method was lack of distance and lack of depth. The tackle was very commonly left to fish for itself whilst the 'piker' did a little roach fishing, or the angler arrived at 11am having been fishing first for his can of livebait. When the livebait ran out he went home or, very rarely, put up a spinning rod.

We mentioned Dennis Pye in Chapter 1. It is of interest that he got around the distance problem by using quite large roach and fishing them under his famous dumbbell float. Properly fished the livebait would search out any required areas both close to and well away from the boat. Dennis did not have a depth problem on the

Dave Steuart with a reservoir 'biggie'. Photo: Dave Steuart

Norfolk Broads, of course, so float-paternostered livebaiting was not for him. Nor did he succumb to the *FG* float, preferring to design his own with his own superior technique.

However, it is important to know what happened elsewhere, because the two methods just described could hardly transform livebaiting or lead to an overall approach to piking. In the 1950s, Barrie, in the north of England, was freelining deadbaits and using the *FG* traditional method for livebaiting. He remembers very well his thought processes that made him change his approach. Firstly, if the deadbait succeeded down on the bottom, where, we now realized, the pike spent much of its time, why not put the livebait there?

The technique was easy: freeline it, just as everything else, including deadbaits, were freelined if you were a real specimen hunter! Secondly, if float fishing was really necessary, then the *FG* certainly wasn't because it was cumbersome, came off the line too easily, and *seemed* to give far too much resistance to the taking pike which, it should be remembered, were rather small in those days.

Freelined Livebait
The big surprise was that the freelined livebait – now lip-hooked rather than in the traditional snap-tackled way – did not continue to pull line off the reel once the fish had swum to the bottom. It was puzzling that it should swim to where the

pike usually were, but not so surprising that having done so it remained very static! Another surprise was that the catch rate quadrupled when compared with shallow-fished livebaits. By then Barrie was using only a (pegged) pilot float rather than past monstrosities; and he had realized that the *FG* float was, anyway, streamlined incorrectly. It should have been set fat-end downwards so that the pointed end disappeared last of all in the event of a take.

At the same time as Dennis Pye was fishing the Broads so was a very young Colin Dyson, experimenting with the use of single hooks, fishing *in* the reed fringes. He eventually abandoned this, but it is of interest that single hooks were investigated so early on. Colin Dyson will be remembered also by many for his outstanding editorship phase at *Coarse Angler*, truly a flagship

magazine for the NFA when Colin was in charge. He regarded himself as a novice in the 1960s but met up with Frank Wright, Dennis Pye, Bill Giles and Reg Sandys and learned his way around the Upper Thurne system. When he left Norfolk for Sheffield he'd already had four 20lb-plus fish, up to 25lb. Then came the *Prymnesium* outbreak, which set back Broads piking dramatically after such devastating fish kills. Colin began piking again in the late 1970s, fishing the Lincolnshire drains, getting two twenties in one day; and in Yorkshire, a twenty from the River Ure. His real tally of big pike began in the 1980s when he fished big gravel pits in Nottingham, getting fifteen in one season, at its best. His grand total was sixty-five over 20lb including two thirty-pounders (one being a fish Barrie caught at 27lb). His best fish on lures was 26½lb.

A twenty-three-pounder in the 1950s, a river fish, and correctly used gaff. Photo: Kay Steuart

LEFT: *Dave Steuart's first ever 20lb fish, the first of many. Note* Fishing Gazette *bung float, and correct use of gaff. Photo: Dave Steuart*

BELOW: *Kay Steuart playing a 21½-pounder in a weirpool. Photo: Dave Steuart*

The 1960s

When *Fishing for Big Pike* was later published in 1971, the freelining technique was outlined, but by the early 1960s Barrie Rickards had added running leads to get distance and had found that this technique worked even better. Note that the Bickerdyke method of paternostering with a fixed lead had not been tried, simply because to put the encumbrance of a fixed lead on the line was against specimen-hunting principles of the time. Even so, ledgered livebait did work well. Ray Webb never got around to it but he did admire the method and was there to net Barrie's first ever twenty-pounder, which fell to the technique.

Something else was happening in the early 1960s, which made all of the above (good thinking though it was) more or less redundant, and today's anglers rarely freeline or ledger livebaits. We have already mentioned Dave Steuart in connection with deadbaiting, but he was also investigating two areas of livebaiting. Firstly, he used large livebaits, becoming convinced that they selected better pike, a view held also by Dennis Pye. Secondly, he had resurrected Norman Hill's paternostering with a float. Dave did write articles in the angling papers and had covered this subject, we think, in a *Fishing Gazette* article. But his technique reached Fenland via two of his friends, Peter Howse and Don Wheeler, who fished regularly with BR and Ray Webb. It quickly became the 'in' method to use, and just to demonstrate the position before it became widespread at the end of the 1960s let us recount Barrie's experience on the Great Ouse Relief Channel. There, in 1965, he was fishing a livebait on the, to him, standard float-paternoster rig, when an angler who had been piking a hundred yards or so along the river came along for a chat. He wanted to know how Barrie managed to fish 3ft deep, cast out into the middle of the Relief Channel, and yet the tackle stayed out there instead of swinging round to the edge with the current flow. Of course, the float was a slider, set against a stop, and a small lead anchored the tackle in place. The angler – a very famous pike angler mark you – was quite dumbfounded, but the very next week had his own system up and running.

The actual rig is shown below. It is almost the same as the float-ledgered deadbait rig of the last chapter except that the lead is on a weaker (paternoster) link, is fixed, and is attached to some part of the wire trace. The float, usually a small pilot float in those days, slid freely on the line but was stopped by a bead above the top swivel (a soft rubber bead ideally) and by a stop knot at the preferred depth. On casting, the float slides down to the bead, and on the lead sinking to the bottom the float slides up to the stop knot. The bait can be fished at any depth or, if there is uncertainty about the depth or if the bottom is irregular, then the lead weight can be such that it sinks the float out of sight and suspends

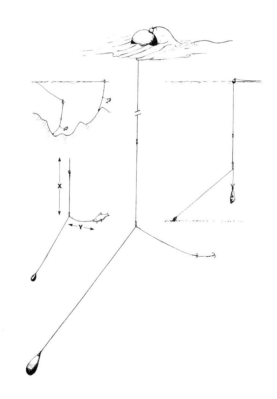

Basic systems used by modern pike anglers. Central figure is of a paternostered float rig with upper trace shown longer than bait trace; top left figures show how the same system can be used in rough terrain with sunken floats (again Y should be less than X); and top right figure is being used for paternostered suspended deadbait.

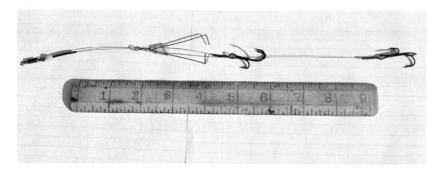

LEFT: *George Higgins'*
deadbait trolling rig.
Photo: George Higgins

BELOW: *A big reservoir*
fish hooked at long range.
Photo: Dave Steuart

the bait at exactly the depth above the bottom that the anger wishes to fish.

It still puzzles us as to why such a vastly improved technique could have got lost between Norman Hill using it and Dave Steuart rediscovering and beginning the popularization of it. Enormous credit goes to Dave Steuart, for this technique has hardly been improved upon since and is now one of the most valuable of piking systems – one could almost argue the most important of all.

You will now fully appreciate why, at the beginning of this chapter, we related the method to the float-fished deadbaiting system. If you are deadbaiting with a sliding float, all you need to do is change the depth stop to the preferred depth, add the appropriate paternoster link and lead, and you have very quickly changed from one deadly technique to the other! You don't need to change the hooks, traces or floats at all.

Dave Steuart became rather famous for this bobble hat, as well as twenty-pound pike! Photo: Dave Steuart

The Angler

New Methods of Using Livebaits

Anglers soon began to use smaller livebaits on float paternoster than Dave Steuart usually did, probably because most anglers did not have access to large baits. It was realized almost immediately that livebaits on a fixed paternoster stayed lively until a pike took them or until they were released, which could never be argued for the old *FG* method of livebaiting. So once again, as in deadbaiting development, the modern, post-1950s pikers had come up with a really good, largely new system, and one moreover that fitted in well with deadbaiting tackle and techniques. Naturally, the same landing and unhooking systems were used by both, and from the late 1960s onwards it became commonplace to see pikers fishing one rod on paternostered livebait and, next to it, another rod on float-ledgered deadbait. If it was a livebait day, then both rods could quickly be set up the same way, and exactly the same obtained if it turned out to be a deadbait day. Furthermore, the day of the pike tackle being fished as a second rod was doomed.

Angling Gear

The angler arrived at the water armed with a tub of livebait, a bag of deadbait and two or more pike rods, plus his chair, rucksack, landing net and so on. He arrived armed to do battle with pike, and equipped for almost every eventuality. In many cases, such as ours, there would also be a spinning rod and a set of lures, but perhaps you can assume that for the rest of the chapter because we'll deal especially with lure fishing in the next.

A Change in the Angler's Start Time

The next question to ask is: *When* did the pike angler arrive? We have already mentioned that pike anglers tended to arrive at the water after they had caught their livebaits, usually not before 11am. But a well-known Sheffield angler, Tag Barnes, fishing in the Lincolnshire drains, reckoned dawn was the time to start piking. His experiences in Lincolnshire convinced him that the best of the pike fishing on any one day might well be all over by 9am. When he wrote about this, in the old A5-size magazine called *Angling*, he was strongly criticized – said to be talking nonsense. But his fellow members of the Northern Specimen Group realized that Tag was not talking nonsense: on angling matters he never did. In the Cambridgeshire fens we found out that, certainly through until December, he was right: dawn was the time to be at the waterside and, quite often, the feeding spell might last for no more than an hour or so, the rest of the day remaining biteless. In those days we would have bags in excess of 100lb by 9am and watch the other pike anglers arriving between 10–11am to face a fruitless day, save perhaps for a jack or two. The big fish feed early. Even during periods when fishing was generally slow it was far more likely that a run would occur at dawn rather than later in the day.

This realization of dawn fishing, which involved arriving well before dawn to be ready and with tackle all set up, was one of the greatest breakthroughs in pike angling, and the basic credit must go to Tag Barnes who first spotted it. Ray Webb, who also influenced Barrie Rickards down in Fenland, in effect led the Northern Specimen Group, often fishing Hornsea Mere in East Yorkshire. By 1964 Ray and Barrie *always* began at dawn whenever possible and by the late 1960s the Cambridgeshire Pike Anglers had spread the word and many were following suit. It may be that this factor is the second most important development in piking, second only to the discovery of static deadbaiting outlined in the last chapter.

OPPOSITE PAGE
TOP: *An 18½lb late-season pike with heavy spawn development, taken on drifter-fished livebait. Photo: Martin Gay*

BOTTOM: *Malcolm Bannister, 1978, with a P.B. from the River Great Ouse of 24lbs 5oz on roach livebait. Photo: Malcolm Bannister*

THIS PAGE
RIGHT: *Graham Marsden, author of one of the most important articles ever on bait fishing (in* Coarse Fisherman, *November 1993, see* text*), with a big one from a Cheshire mere. Photo: Graham Marsden*

BELOW: *Barrie Rickards doing what he does best: being bone idle behind deadbait rods on a Fenland river. Photo: Barrie Rickards*

So anglers were arriving pre-dawn, armed with all their bait for the day, including livebait caught previously and stored. This last activity had always gone on on the Norfolk Broads for example, but now it became much more commonplace. Anglers had large aerated tanks in their garages or back gardens and these were stocked up with small fish caught or trapped from a variety of productive waters. A variety of species were useful as bait, such as tiny bream, the usual roach and dace, but also perch and small chub. And always there were rudd, gudgeon and ruffe and occasionally bleak too. The best baits of all were found to be small chub, followed perhaps by tiny bream, but with the float-paternostered systems

in use it didn't matter too much what the bait was because it would stay lively until taken by a pike – and then would often swim off after the strike! Efficient livebait storage systems enabled pike anglers to fish all day with great efficiency. Today all this is illegal. Baits must be caught on the day in question, on the water in question, or be supplied by the authorities responsible for the fishing – often in the form of small rainbow trout, which are also excellent livebaits. The real point of the livebait movement bans, indeed the only valid point, is to prevent the spread of species. Certainly movement of baits has never been proven to have spread diseases, that being the downside of commercial fish-farming only.

ABOVE: *Barrie Rickards demonstrating how pike were weighed up until the 1980s. Photo: Barrie Rickards*

LEFT: *Dave Steuart netting a twenty-pounder with early triangular landing net (and knotted net material). Photo: Dave Steuart*

Whether it is very important to attempt to prevent the spread of coarse fish species is debateable, but the upshot of these restrictions is that far more deadbaiting than ever is now done with livebaiting a somewhat second-string technique – if they are available, yes; if not, get the deadbaits out. It is a real restriction on piking because there are times and waters where livebaits are by far the best baits.

The Roll-Up Bag

A little earlier we alluded to the preparedness of the angler arriving pre-dawn. What happened, once the crucial nature of dawn fishing was recognized, was interesting, because before dawn, tackling up would be difficult – is difficult. Laurie Manns and Barrie, in the Fens, started arriving at the water with the whole tackle rig set up. That is, the reels were on the rods, the line threaded through the rings, the floats and end rigs were on. All one had to do to start fishing was put the bait on, or perhaps a lead on the paternoster. We could be fishing within a minute on one rod and within three minutes on two rods, Laurie used to bring his rods wrapped up in an old mac, ready for action. Barrie simply had them loose, risking tangles, which you didn't need before daylight. (Remember, too, that in those days, the use of torches was frowned upon, being against Walkerian specimen-hunting principles.)

Rian Tingay, Fenland tiger and pike angler extraordinary, seeing what Laurie and Barrie were up to with roll-up macs, went one better and got a saddle maker in Littleport to make a roll-up rod bag in green canvas. It was such a success that within a few months several Fenland pikers were using them. It is worth emphasizing just what an improvement those were upon the old fishing holdall, which was based upon the golf-bag principle. This meant that rods were pushed in, and rings were damaged. They were totally hopeless for the made-up rods, which we were now using in order to catch the dawn feed without hiccups. The roll-up holdall protects the rods much better, enables the reel spool to be placed in a pocket, and also holds rod rests, landing net pole and brolly. The advantages also include the fact that

the angler finding his way along the banks in the dark only has a rucksack and roll-up holdall as main items, and two free hands, one of which can be used for the livebait bucket. This approach to piking was both more efficient and is in tune with the modern approach. All this is quite different to the piking inherited by pike anglers in the late 1950s and early 1960s. In terms of the roll-up holdall, credit should go to Rian Tingay and the other Fenland pikers.

Incidentally, Barrie tried quite hard to get the tackle trade to manufacture the roll-up holdall, but was met with almost a total lack of interest and understanding of what was happening – all except for Bob Church, who was then in the early days of the tackle trade. Eventually, Barrie publicized the roll-up in *Fishing for Big Pike*.

The original roll-up canvas rod holdall.
Photo: Barrie Rickards

This made the idea readily available to everyone, but at the same obviated any chance of patenting the method. Within a decade tens of thousands of roll-up holdalls had been sold, although most were rather inferior to the original in canvas. Malcolm had his made by the local saddler.

The Rod Quiver

Another good idea, almost a reversion to the old, bag style, was the quiver, designed originally, we think, by Terry Eustace. It looks just like a Robin Hood quiver for arrows, but with an extra pocket low on the outside into which the several (made-up) rod butts rested. The rods could be folded in two, but fully made up and *with reels attached*, at the beginning of the day. Later in the day the rods can be transported without breaking them down at all. Simply stick the rod butts in the low pocket, fix the middle parts of the rods with a rod-tie positioned near the top of the quiver, stick the brolly and rod rests in the main quiver pocket, and off you go. It's all very quick, and very efficient. We use both the roll-up full holdall and the quiver, depending upon whether we plan to be static for half a day, or on the move. Terry Eustace, of course, is a top-class pike angler and one who led the investigations in the 1970s into the problems of so-called gassed-up pike, eventually concluding that a fish sunk deep and/or kept still and quiet eventually recovered. Martin Gay and Barrie had one experience of this on a shallow reservoir – so there was no question of the pike coming up from deep water – and found that the fish recovered in a couple of hours having been propped up carefully with sticks stuck in the bottom in about one foot of water. The pike swam off quite easily in the end and certainly never appeared again either that day or for the three following.

To jump forward just a little, by the late 1980s the carp angling boom had led to the development of another type of rod holdall, which also took the full reel, in pockets. These are not entirely suitable for winter piking but they were adopted and roll-ups went into decline, reappearing only in 2005 in a small way. They are still the best kit for the job.

Places to Fish

On this road to improved piking chance plays a part, such as the fact that after the major freeze-up in 1963, pike were getting bigger again. They were also becoming more widespread as gravel pits were dug, and also as anglers in general stopped killing pike (only gradually, but it all helped). So an understanding of pike feeding habits coupled with the more holistic approach did lead to improved results. Whereas in the immediate past only certain places produced big pike (for example, the Norfolk Broads, Hornsea Mere, Slapton Ley) now big pike were turning up everywhere, not least in the Cambridgeshire Fens.

But more was yet to come. The idea – very real idea – of pike feeding at dawn wasn't the whole story. People like Ray Webb, especially, were analysing catches in great detail. It was Ray who really hammered home Tag Barnes' dawn feeding discovery, and Barrie remembers Ray, in 1960–62 in particular, re-jigging their joint trips so that they started at dawn. Of all anglers, Ray was probably the most perceptive in recognizing patterns.

Feeding Patterns

His next great discovery was that of feeding patterns. Earlier in this chapter we hinted that dawn feeding persisted until around December when the water temperatures dropped. Ray noted that whilst things might be slow at dawn now, there was still a short feeding spell at some stage of the day, often around midday. It was crucial to identify this feeding spell, usually no more than an hour, even though it varied from water to water. Now, older anglers were fully aware that pike could be caught in the middle of the day in winter, which is one of the reasons why they arrived at 11am rather than at dawn. It just shows how easily one can get things wrong because they waited for the first frosts before commencing their pike fishing, they were quite unaware of other feeding times in September to early December.

Anglers did not believe Ray's claims of feeding patterns, but to Barrie he proved it repeatedly. He recalls one of the earliest days on the Relief Channel with Ray. Ray had fished for five days

Barrie playing a good fish on static deadbait (sardine). Photo: Barrie Rickards

previously and every run had come between 10–11.30am. Barrie was himself sceptical about these claims but on that day they had five runs, the first at 10.05am and the last at 11.15am. No runs at dawn, and no runs later in the day even though they fished into the dark. Most anglers today reckon that feeding patterns are extremely important. And, of course, they provide encouragement when things seemed slow. So feeding patterns were written up in *Fishing for Big Pike* and seemed to receive general acceptance much more quickly than dawn fishing did.

Guidelines to Finding Pike – 'The Hotspots'

If we may now recap just a little. We have, now, a very efficient pike angler. Capable of arriving at a water before dawn, ready to use live- and deadbait at the same time, fishing only for pike. Naturally he is aware of dawn feeding, and of feeding patterns and he has all the pike gear for the job, unlike the pre-1960s when almost nothing really suitable was sold. But what if there are no pike in the swim? How can he tell that? What are the guidelines? This was an area where tremendous progress was made in the 1960s, and once again much of what was discovered was down to Ray Webb, at least initially. Many anglers realized, of course, that to catch big pike you had to fish waters that held them. In the 1960s many waters, following post catastrophic freeze-ups and the kill-all-pike mentality pervading the country as a whole, big pike waters were not easy to find, except the most famous ones. So anglers headed for the Norfolk Broads, for Hornsea Mere in East Yorkshire, for Slapton

A big reservoir pike nears the margins. Photo: Derek Gibson

Ley and Bosherston in the south, or the Hampshire Avon. A few of us were fishing clay pits in Yorkshire and catching double-figure fish, and some of us were exploring the hundreds of miles of waterways in the Cambridgeshire Fens. Tag Barnes and others were trying the Lincolnshire Fens. No anglers, at that time, were going to Scotland and only a few, such as Fred Buller and Ray Webb, were going to Ireland.

So anglers even in the late 1950s and 1960s chased the known big pike waters, whilst others explored new regions: it was ever thus! In addition, there were certain rules of thumb which enabled pikers to find pike, such as looking for dense common reed beds, or side streams entering a river or broad, or weir pools, or sunken trees: in short, features. On any one water such places became heavily fished or, as we would now recognize it, seriously overfished. When we tried new waters, and Ray Webb and Barrie spent a lot of time doing just that, we found that such features could be relied upon to produce a

fish or two. But that is the correct phrase to use: features provide a fish or two because they are good ambush points, but they do not necessarily produce many fish, the big fish, or fish all that regularly.

The answer slowly came to Ray Webb when he was fishing waters in East Yorkshire, including Hornsea Mere and, slightly later (1963/64), when in Fenland and the Norfolk Broads. He spent some time persuading Barrie of his discoveries, but after a year's demonstrating in practical ways he convinced him finally, and Barrie had to accept that *hotspots* existed on many, if not all waters. Hotspots are small areas, sometimes no more than 30yd long, where almost all the big pike on a water spend *most* of their time, and where they can be caught regularly and in large numbers. Hotspots can also be recognized by the fact that outside the hotspot very few big pike will ever be caught except when the whole pike population in the water is on a feeding, hunting frenzy, and that is rare to experience. Fishing up to half a dozen anglers on a stretch of drain, the Cambridgeshire Pike Anglers proved again and again that to be outside the hotspot was a waste of time. Both Ray and Barrie came to the conclusion that the big pike were more or less resident in the spot that, as often as not, was totally featureless – no gravel bar, no sunken tree, no stonework.

Searching the Banks

The approach adopted by Ray and Barrie was to creep into position before dawn, set up the rods, and fish quietly for the whole day if necessary. Before a hotspot was actually discovered they'd search the banks day-by-day, week-by-week, until they found it. Once it was discovered, huge bags could be expected, and on many occasions bags in excess of 100lb were achieved, and quite frequently bags over 200lb. These would include anything up to a dozen big double-figure fish and twenty-pounders too. Hotspots don't take kindly to overfishing and if that happens they really only last one to three seasons. In contrast, Barrie has been fishing one hotspot, on a private water where there is little pressure, and the hotspot has remained in exactly the same place for thirty years. On another water, this time public water, he has fished such a hotspot for twenty-seven years. These still produce big fish regularly and big bags fairly frequently, and both dawn feeding and other feeding patterns are identified from time to time.

It has been argued by some that the pike are not actually resident in these places, but visit them to feed. This very reasonable idea doesn't really work, because it implies that the food fish stay in one place all the time, which is patently untrue. Far more likely is that cyprinid shoals pass by or through the hotspots at intervals and incite the pike to feed. The 'visiting' theory does not explain why big pike are not caught fairly frequently outside the hotspot. Martin Gay, fishing the Kent gravel pits, did find that the pike moved about quite a bit and *did* visit certain points of certain bars. Later on he realized that those pits also had real hotspots, and when he found them he had some large catches. This is a

form of hotspot, which he would concede is a little bit different and is feature-related. A good case might be the valve towers on Abberton Reservoir in Essex. Here the brickwork features attract so many cyprinids that a good number of big pike are always going to be in residence there. However, fishing restrictions at Abberton meant that it was impossible to discover if these really were classic hotspots. Martin and Barrie fished another reservoir, which also had valve tower attendees: but this reservoir also had a tiny hotspot, miles from anywhere and discovered by Barrie from which they caught huge bags of fish within 10yd of the bank, and quite a few twenty-pounders too. To this day only three anglers know of this hotspot – two, if you remember that Martin is no longer with us and may now be sitting upon a cloud watching us.

On yet another southern reservoir, but quite a small one this time, Martin and Barrie took good pike close to the reservoir outlet brickwork and gates that dominated one end of the water. Yet the real hotspot was a 10yd-length of bank about 200yd from the outlet system, and here the pike could be caught in numbers, frequently, and to good size, by fishing perhaps 20ft from the bank. Very careful plumbing of this whole bank revealed not a single feature of any kind, but merely a steep slope down to 12ft or so at around 10ft out from the bank. The hotspot remained for several seasons until they lost the fishing rights. It probably still exists.

You can be in denial as regards hotspots, and still catch pike of course, but find one, recognize it over a period of a season or so, and you will then *know* the reality of them. Hotspots, as will be clear from the above, are hard to find because they are few in number on any water, and are small. To find them involves fishing a water regularly, moving position each time to some sort of plan (putting great reliance on results at dawn, for example), perhaps leap-frogging along the bank, a technique often use by the Cambridgeshire Pike Anglers. And there is another way too, and that is to search a water with lures. Basil Chilvers, alas no longer with us, used this technique in the fens in the 1960s: having located a few double-figure pike with lure, he would move in the following week with baits to test the area. You need to be careful if doing this, because there is no point lure fishing late, if the fish went off the feed at 9am. You need to be in at dawn and to fish seriously, rather than half-heartedly chucking a lure around whilst your deadbait rods fish 'on the buzzers' some distance away! Leave the bait rods at home for this approach.

Tracking Pike Movements
It might be assumed from the foregoing that we do not think pike move around very much, but this would be incorrect; for much of the time, most of the year, they do not. Various tracking programmes, involving tags or radio transmitters, have been used to see where pike go, and it is clear that they go a long way. But how real is this? In the tagging programmes in which we have been involved, recapture of tagged fish has been rare. Yet recapture of pike in hotspots is common. Does the hydrodynamic drag of a tag or transmitter make them go walkabout? It is quite possible. Think about it. When a pike takes a deadbait and feels the drag of the lead, it sets off on a run, which quite often shows no sign of stopping. You can try this with a tied-on bait (that is, no hooks) and you will be staggered just how far they will go. And remember too, the lead may actually be tapping the flanks of the pike as it swims! Pike do migrate, it is true, but maybe not as much as these experiments imply. Malcolm has found that the Crossens Drain pike do move about and quite some distance too, and that the stay in one swim approach is often better than leap-frogging along the drain. They migrate, in particular, to their spawning ground, and at these times the hotspots may be quite empty of fish. Those pikers who have observed the spawning areas can do really well by fishing close to them before the spawning activity starts. When it does the pike will just ignore your baits, and you too.

Enough of hotspots. We have been deliberately introducing slightly more controversial matters as this chapter has progressed, not least because it reflects truthfully the great progress in piking and the willingness of anglers to question what went before: the modern pike angler is really empowered by tackle and techniques, yet continues to question and probe. So let us now look at another matter.

Barometric Pressure
This may raise the blood pressure of some! There can be absolutely no doubt at all that changes in barometric pressure affect the animal world in dramatic fashion. The onset of very thundery weather, with its accompanying pressure changes, can cause immediate headaches in humans, and bizarre behaviour in animals both on land and in water. In the late 1970s Malcolm and Barry Burton caught a large number of pike during a very heavy thunderstorm. A large shoal of bream passed though their swims, rolling on the top as they passed by. This was very quickly followed by what at the time seemed almost all the pike in the Crossens Drain. Malcolm has never seen its like to this day. If you know a water that is full of eels, and it's not too deep, go and observe them during the build up to a thunderstorm. You will see them vertical in the water and undergoing strange gyrations at times. Maybe they have headaches. It is often argued, by the anti-barometric-pressure anglers, that water is incompressible and so changes in air pressure will have no effect on water. This is only partly true. For example, increased air pressure (high pressure) will put more oxygen into the surface layers of water, and hence to the water as a whole. Anyone involved in active fishing, such as a fly fisherman, knows full well that a rise in the barometer results in more activity on the part of trout. And why shouldn't it if more oxygen is available to them?

Many years ago David Marlborough drew Barrie's attention to a scientific work in France, in which fish (mostly trout) had had their behaviours observed over a long period. Now the importance of this work was that it was carried out in a large tank, *inside* a building, so that the effects of wind, rain, fog, temperature, even sunshine, could be eliminated. The tank was very large, filling the entire ground floor of a moderate-sized institute

Derek Gibson with a 31¼lb fish – and half a head. Photo: Derek Gibson

building. The observers noted that the trout became very active, and keen to feed near the surface, when the barometer was high, and became sluggish and bottom hugging when the barometer was low. They attributed such activity to barometric pressure not least because the activity did not seem to coincide with the lunar cycle.

However, the moon *must* have an effect on fish, and on barometric pressure too in some circumstances. Think about the tidal effect in sea fishing and any tidal waterway. We'll return to the subject of the moon's influence towards the end of the book, because thinking on this subject is of very modern times as far as pike angling is concerned. It is not our immediate concern.

In the early 1960s Barrie had been aware of the influence of barometric pressure on tench, eels and trout, from his own fishing, but had not equated pike and pressure, until a moment of illumination when he and Ray Webb were pike fishing in the fens. The insight, as so often, came from Ray. They'd had almost a week of fishing during a real low-pressure system. The weather had been cold, sometimes foggy, a little snow, rain and sun; and the fishing had been slow, with livebaits ignored and a few fish on deadbaits only. Quite suddenly, within an hour, the fish came on the feed and took anything thrown at them, dead or alive. Some big fish were caught, and plenty of them. The weather had not changed at all; they were still frozen stiff (in the inadequate clothing of those times); but several hours later the weather went mild and a southwesterly breeze started during the night. Careful checking with the local RAF station showed that the barometer had begun to rise steeply just as the fish came on the feed. Coincidence in angling just wasn't in Ray's vocabulary and from that day on he became fully convinced that Barrie was right about pressure changes in angling, and he set about, in his very thorough way, analysing catches against barometric pressure. He used the charts published in newspapers, but he also rang the RAF frequently. They must have got fed up. Incidentally, Martin Gay also used to use the RAF, because they had very accurate and detailed weather reports. Perhaps the two of them put undue strain on the system because if you do this now you have to pay for the information.

Conclusions Regarding the Effects of Barometric Pressure

The conclusions we came to, over a five-year period, were as follows:

- The actual barometric pressure figure is not the important factor, by and large.
- A sudden drop in barometric pressure sends fish off the feed.
- A rise in barometric pressure makes fish active and prepared to feed on anything, dead or alive.
- A prolonged and steady low pressure results, after the initial fall is past, in pike feeding on deadbaits on the bottom. (*Small* pike may feed on lures and livebaits at this time, whilst the big pike scavenge round the bottom.)
- During high-pressure regimes, especially near the beginning of one, pike will select livebaits in preference to bottom-fished deadbaits. Suspended deadbaits may be taken in preference to livebaits, or vice versa, or they may take both.
- In deeper waters, say upwards of 6–8ft, the distinction between effectiveness of live versus dead is more marked. In shallow drains exceptions to the above 'rules' occur, but they *are* exceptions.

None of us would argue that other factors could override the role of barometric pressure on occasions. Obvious examples are exceptional floods, with raging torrents of water; pollution; the fresh introduction of 10,000 naïve troutlings, and so on. But as a generalization, it does work and, along with some of the other discoveries we have outlined in this chapter, it can influence one's approach to a day's pike fishing or, more particularly perhaps, to half a day's piking. If you can get an afternoon off work, but realize that the feeding pattern is in the morning, then you could be exceptionally conscientious and stay at work! If the barometer is rocketing upwards, as it often does as a thaw takes place, then forget work completely and go fishing, making sure you have plenty of livebaits. Barrie and Malcolm only deadbait these days, for no other reason than a general bone-idle disposition, and the inadequacy of using only one method has been brought home to them many times. The abandoning of livebaiting, on ethical grounds by Richard Walker, may not have adversely affected Richard's piking results for some reason, but they have certainly reduced Barrie's results. Of course, Barrie lure fishes too, but as a deadbait, lure and pike fly angler, cannot really consider himself a truly holistic pike angler as argued in this chapter.

In this chapter we have outlined how the very efficient overall approach to piking – an holistic approach – evolved. Obviously we operate this way ourselves, except that Barrie usually only deadbaits and lure fishes these days. But many successful anglers adopted this approach, which is really very, very adaptable to the circumstances. If you read Bill Palmer's superb book *Dimples to Wrinkles* you will see exactly what we mean. In his foreword to this book Martin Gay wrote, 'If readers … hope to find details of secret methods or magic bait they will be disappointed. But if they are looking for the secret of success they will find it'. Exactly so: Bill Palmer is the epitome of the holistic approach and one of the greatest pike anglers. We now want to look at lure fishing itself in order to make a judgement. Has it also progressed as successfully as bait fishing?

4 LURE FISHING

This branch of the sport has developed in a very interesting way compared with the rest of piking. It would not be easy to argue, for example, that the sport took off in the late 1950s and early 1960s, as did the rest of piking. When we dealt with Charles Thurlow-Craig in *The Ten Greatest Pike Anglers*, he formed the subject of our very last chapter: his classic book *Spinners Delight* was published in 1951 and it brought us, in effect, right to the coverage of the present book. But reflect a little, Thurlow-Craig was ahead of his time on lure fishing: he used multipliers, made his own rods and lures, and explored many aspects of lure fishing. In a way he was extremely modern. At the same time, live-baiting was as it had been for hundreds of years, notwithstanding Norman Hill's work, and dead-baiting had not been re-invented. So he really was ahead of the game. Fred J. Taylor was greatly inspired by Thurlow-Craig, which explains why he continued as a successful lure fisherman as well as being a deadbait enthusiast.

Prior to Thurlow-Craig, lure fishing had been a bit of spinning or trolling of spoons such as the Colorado and the Kidney spoon or the Norwich spoon – and that too had gone on for a very long time. It's odd that Thurlow-Craig's approach did not catch on, and this may have been that relatively few anglers read his books, and certainly he would not get the media exposure of today. Nor did he cover spinning, or indeed angling, in his legendary *Sunday Express* column 'Up Country'. Had he done so, perhaps later spinning might have had a different history.

Thurlow-Craig made some mistakes, such as disparaging lures from the USA: he considered his own homemade ones better, which they were probably not. And he considered lure fishing the only sporting method of piking, a philosophically weak argument, and not one that would find favour with the modern holistic piker of the preceding chapter. He also fished in the Welsh Borders, not at the time a Mecca for pike fishing. Had he fished on the Norfolk Broads, once again the history of lure fishing might be different.

Lure Fishing in the 1950s

When Barrie began lure fishing early in the 1950s he hadn't heard of Thurlow-Craig, even though *Spinners Delight* had just been published, and what he found was a very basic sport. Fixed spool reels were only just coming into general use at a price that ordinary anglers could afford, and buying multipliers was really out of the question for most anglers. Rods were rather stiff, except for one or two quality rods from the likes of Hardy – again, way beyond the pocket of the ordinary angler. A few short bait-casting rods were around, and the man who taught Barrie his early lure fishing, Mike O'Donnell, used one of these, in built cane, with a fixed spool reel, monofil of around 8–10lb BS and, eventually, a wire trace. Wire traces were quite hawser-like, black, and many anglers, Barrie included, fished without them until the inevitable happened: after landing any number of small to medium pike, a big one was hooked, which had engulfed the whole lure, and a bite-off resulted. It was a salutary lesson Barrie did not forget. He converted a Tom Watsons' 9ft so-called 'boy's rod' so that it had a good handle and could be used for spinning. Tom Watson was himself impressed with the conversion but declined to go into production of the rod! The rod was stiff enough to set trebles, and bendy enough to cast and play fish; but we are talking fish up to 12lb, not monsters.

Many anglers made their own lures, possibly rather better lures than did Thurlow-Craig, and Barrie had considerable success on his floating divers (nowadays termed crankbaits for some reason). The actual choice of lures available was not great because lures from the USA did not appear in any numbers until the mid-1960s, and those that were available were extremely expensive to buy, and to lose. Barrie made the same mistake as Thurlow-Craig, and dismissed them as angler-catchers rather than fish-catchers. This appraisal was reached after spending the day on some borrow pits in East Yorkshire in the company of three adults who had all the gear, including boxes of American lures. They didn't have a fish all day whereas Barrie had several, all on his limited selection of old-fashioned lures.

Types of Lure

So what lures *were* available to the average angler keen on doing a little spinning? Firstly, there were some single and jointed plugs, usually blue in colour, and armed with a couple of soft double hooks. They caught fish, but any dampness (for example, water!) cracked the paint layers in no time, and they soon became brown wood lacking any colour, and they were relatively expensive.

Secondly there were mackerel spinners – obviously borrowed from the world of sea fishing. These were, and are, good lures in shallow, weedy pits and Mike O'Donnell and Barrie used them to good effect all over the East and West Ridings of Yorkshire, catching double-figure pike occasionally. They cast well and fish well, and they are cheap. They also tangle the line infuriatingly unless you have an anti-kink lead or vane on the trace – more expense. More on anti-kink vanes later on.

Norwich spoons were hard to come by, but Colorado and Kidney spoons were readily available, cast well and caught fish. Even on the small lakes a small Colorado caught Barrie a great many pike, and perch too. You could also buy the game angler's metal minnows in a range of sizes, and wagtails made of bird quill or rubber: all these worked and they also twisted up the line no end.

Finally there was a small French plug of rubber called a Plucky Bait, and this was possibly the best lure available in the 1950s. Regrettably it went out of production. You could make your own plugs, and these usually worked very well once you had the balance correct so that they retrieved well. And you could make your own spoons out of dessert-spoons. This did give rise to what one might term social problems! Spoons were not that cheap in those days, tended to come in well-guarded sets, and when they went missing investigations were held. Should the spoon be discovered on the end of a line, rather than adjacent to apple pie, then crises ensued. They worked really well! Home-made spoons cast well and caught well, could be fished at any depth, and painted any colour. When Barrie was a youngster his father was discovered by his mother, drilling holes in the ends of one of the family spoons in order to convert it to its more important role in life, namely catching pike. You can imagine the resulting furore.

We have not painted this picture of the primitive state of lure fishing in the early 1950s just for effect. That really was the situation: a few brands of long-established lures, rather an inadequate range of (affordable) rods, and a persisting idea that spinning only caught small pike anyway.

Let's examine this last point more fully. The view that lure fishing catches only small pike is still with us today, but rapidly losing force as an argument. Dead- and livebait fishing was so improved from the 1960s that it left lure fishing behind, stuck in the past. Yet not many years later Barrie did a calculation based on his catches of 20lb-plus pike on lures and baits, and came to the conclusion that lure fishing was just as effective at getting big pike as were baits. Most anglers, including some very famous ones, didn't agree, but today most would probably hold the same view. It is, however, necessary to compare like with like. One day with three bait-rods is equivalent to three rod-days with the lure rod, so that bait-fishing results need, in this example, to be divided by three. Once you do that you soon realize just how effective lure fishing really is and, like livebait fishing, it also produces plenty of makeweight fish. Lure fishing – not even trolling – can ever be considered boring, whereas some do find sitting behind static dead-bait rods so. Not us, we hasten to add.

RIGHT: *A giant pike from the Lake District. Photo: Dave Kelbrick*

BELOW: *A large pike with spectacular spotting. Photo: Dave Kelbrick*

Lure Fishing in the 1960s – a Boom Time

So there we were, in the early 1960s, bait fishing forging ahead thanks to Fred J. Taylor and others, and lure fishing rather static, in the doldrums almost. Then along came Messrs Wagstaffe and Reynolds. Fred Wagstaffe and Bob Reynolds formed a very successful team of pikers, fishing the Fens, the Norfolk Broads and Ireland especially. At roughly the same time the Norfolk tackle dealer Ken Latham, who had a big shop in Potter Heigham, began importing hundreds of lures from the USA. These included such surface gems as the Crazy Crawler, which excited a great deal of attention. And there was the Creek Chub range, some of which were so big they would dwarf some of the pike being caught. Malcolm bought some of Ken Latham's last stocks. The fact is that because of the activities of Fred and Bob, and the articles they wrote (especially for *Angling Times*), anglers realized that American lures really did work, and in many circumstances were much better than their British counterparts, if that is, there were any counterparts. These two anglers caused great excitement in the piking world and a bit of a boom in lure fishing began. For the first time since Thurlow-Craig, pike anglers fished surface lures for pike as well as much superior floating divers. Some quite good spoons were available too, the Piker being one, if a little flighty on casting. Encouraged by the terrible duo, anglers made their own lures out of broom handles and chair legs (which also led to social problems on occasion!) and learnt how to put weed guards on them and stinger trebles. Big pike were caught and Fred and Bob made no secret of their views that lures could catch big pike regularly.

Looking back it is strange that this boom in lure angling eventually faded out. In part this was because the two chief protagonists left the scene as though bored with it. But it was also that old, old problem, namely that bait fishing was going through such amazing developments that it tended to push lure fishing into the background. Also, it was known that some of the very best catches made by Fred Wagstaffe and Bob Reynolds were not made on lures, but on baits. That alone tended to knock the shine off the lure-fishing ball. Even so, the adventures of Fred and Bob on their boat 'Black Pig', in western Ireland, will live for a long time in the minds of many pikers, bait- and lure-fisher alike.

Lure Fishing in the 1970s – Development of Lure Fishing

It was a strange time for some of us to see this apparent demise of a splendid part of the sport. It is probably fair to say that the Wagstaffe/Reynolds lure-fishing boom did not survive the early 1970s. At least, not in its exuberant form. But it *did* survive in a fashion. Those anglers such as Barrie who had always lure fished, continued to do so, and were joined by others such as Gordon Burton, now famous but then much less so. Ray Webb himself continued lure fishing in Ireland, taking a 29lb fish from the River Suck. As with all things, Ray got things down to a fine art when it came to the use of lures from boats, whether casting or trolling. Trolling in Ireland had continued, of course, in quite uninterrupted fashion with anglers like Fred Buller doing very

well in southern Ireland and, increasingly, the Northern Ireland Pikers in their own neck of the woods and on Lough Allen.

Perhaps this rather quiet time in lure fishing, the 1970s, is best summed up in two books written by Barrie and Ken Whitehead (Deryck Swift). Firstly there was *Plugs and Plug Fishing* in 1976, followed by *Spinners, Spoons, and Wobbled Baits* in 1977. These books dealt with all the old-style lure fishing, encompassed the Wagstaffe/Reynolds era (because the authors were part of it), and really took us right up to where we were then in terms of tackle and techniques – as well as all those exotic lures and their uses. The omnibus edition of these two books, a decade later, brought everything up to date and even included an underwater analysis of lure flash patterns (using the aquatic equivalent of a wind tunnel and Ken Whitehead's photographic skills) as well as pike fly-fishing. They were up-to-date books, ahead of their time in some respects, useful today to some extent, but in truth were not much beyond the Wagstaffe/Reynolds period, useful though they undoubtedly were. There had been an earlier book (1970), *Spinning for Pike,* by R.C.R. Barder, but it was not altogether about spinning and it mentions neither Wagstaffe nor Reynolds, being rather of the old-fashioned form of lure fishing referred to earlier. Fred J. Taylor made a contribution to that book and he was one of those anglers keeping alive the spirit of lure fishing. Lure fishing was in stasis for a decade; it had taken one small step forward and then faltered. What happened next is still with us and growing.

Lure Fishing in the 1980s – Further Expansion

The real revolution in lure fishing, although helped on a little by all the foregoing, took place from the late 1980s onwards. It has been a quite unparalleled and undreamt of expansion, with a phenomenal range of lures and tackle now available and a host of quite new techniques. So what on earth happened?

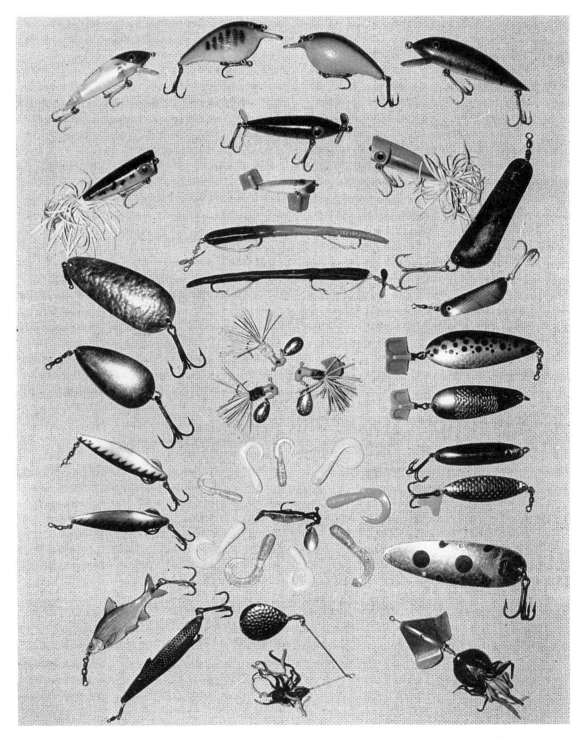

A range of smaller plugs, spoons, jigs and spinnerbaits, part of the vast range now available to the lure fisherman.
Photo: Barrie Rickards

It may not be quite so easy to answer that question! We are talking about something that began in the mid-1980s and took off a year or two later. Charlie Bettell in his book *The Art of Lure Fishing* (1994) says that 'something happened' in 1986, in the form of the T G Lure Fishing Championships – the very first national lure-fishing championship held at Ardingly Reservoir. Subsequent championships were held at Thorpe Park.

Barrie finished thirteenth in the first Thorpe Park competition; and he was awarded the golden *kussamo* (Professor) spoon for his contributions to lure angling. Charlie may well have put his finger on the trigger for the next and biggest ever explosion in lure angling. John Milford and

A 19½lb fish goes airborne. Photo: George Higgins

Graham Easton owned T & G Tackle and imported huge quantities of lures from the USA. They enthused about them, gave talks, seminars and teach-ins and ran competitions. Some of us tested lures and reported on them for the company. In short, it was a very vibrant atmosphere. Every time Barrie gave a lecture, organized by John and Graham, it was packed and the enthusiasm infectious. This had never happened before in spite of all the efforts of Fred Wagstaffe and Bob Reynolds. Sales of the lures took off, far in excess of the Ken Latham days, and before too long other, small companies began marketing lures too, and creating new ones. Kiltly lures, for example came up with their Flying C (short for condom) and some very exotic spoons. Also in the forefront were New World Lures and Pearce Lures and associated loosely with those firms were very successful lure anglers such as Chris Leibbrandt and Steve Gould, the latter taking five 20lb pike in one morning on Llandegfedd Reservoir. That catch on lures certainly opened the eyes of the angling world to lure fishing.

However you look at this one, it seems that the only anglers you can credit with starting it all off were John Milford and Graham Easton, assisted by lots of their friends. True, Gordon Burton was now making a bit of a name for himself, deservedly, and the rest of the 'old lads' were still lure fishing and writing about it, in Barrie's case a long-running monthly article in the magazine, *Coarse Fisherman* ... But it was the sudden increase in availability of a great many new lures, the media hype that went with it, and the shear buzz of excitement going through the world of pike angling that got it going.

The Range of Lures in the 1980s

Perhaps it might be a good idea if we gave a brief breakdown now of the range of lures available at that stage, the mid to late 1980s. Remember it immediately followed the omnibus edition of the Rickards and Whitehead update on lure fishing. The change was rapid and the range of lures quadrupled in a season.

For the first time there was a range of seriously deep divers, that is those lures that have a big, horizontal diving blade at the head of the lure. Some of these seemed to dive almost vertically and they are just as quick to rise when you stop cranking the reel handle. In the Fens we found we could fish some deep holes, with a nice-looking plug, in a way that we hadn't been able to do before. Of course, they plough into the near bank if your judgement is bad, but you soon learn.

Surface lures were available in the previous lure fishing boom, but attention was mostly focused on the Crazy Crawler. Good lure that it is, there were many more available, and in this 1980s boom they arrived in numbers from the USA via TG lures. Amongst the best of these, some had propellers either at the front of the lure or at the rear, or both, such as the Sinner Spinner, Torpedoes, Sputterbug and so on. Others were surface poppers like the Trouble Maker or Lucky 13. Malcolm fished the Lucky 13 to good effect much like you would a 'Big S' running through the top 3ft of water. A more or less direct alternative to the Crazy Crawler was the Jitterbug range. Some of them were around when Ken Whitehead and Barrie were writing, and they included them in their books: Ken had done extremely well with

the Lucky 13 at that stage, but the range is better covered by Charlie Bettell in his 1994 Crowood volume, *The Art of Lure Fishing*.

Surface Jerkbaits

Also around in the 1980s were some small, surface jerkbaits (of which more a little later) such as the Zara Spook, the Woodwalker and other Zara brands. These were also good lures for Ken and Barrie, but they did not reach their acme until the 1990s perhaps. They were not known as jerkbaits at that stage, and they were essentially rather small, but effective, lures used on or close to the surface and jerked so that they disturbed the surface layers of water. Fishing them is quite an art, and the actual technique has to be modified from water to water because the pike react differently on different venues.

Crankbaits

Another name change, which we do not fully understand, is that from 'floating divers' of the Rickards/Whitehead era, to the 'crankbait' of today. The latter term certainly came in from the USA in the TG Lures' time, and also now covers

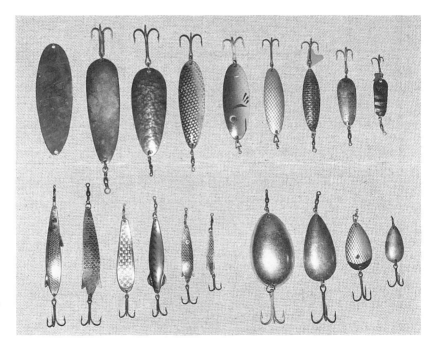

A range of spoons including homemade copper spoons. Photo: Barrie Rickards

those divers that sink slowly, or are of neutral buoyancy, but which dive further on retrieve. Perhaps these would be better included with countdown lures, which sink fairly quickly before they are retrieved from the desired depth. It is just possible that the great majority of plugs are crankbaits: almost every manufacturer produces quite a range of floating divers. We once had our firm favourites, such as the Creek Chub range, but now the choice is large, and they all work well and perform well from time to time.

Jigs

Then there are the jigs. Back in the 1960s Barrie used Rapala jigs – just about the only ones available – quite successfully. His trick was to fish them off bridges, such as those many bridges along the Sixteen Foot River in the Cambridge Fens. But they worked anywhere, sinking and then being retrieved with a vibrating motion. By the 1970s a bigger range was available including worms and other rubber jigs. In the 1980s yet more arrived from the USA, some being striking look-alikes for prey fish, such as small trout or minnows.

In the mid-1980s Barrie worked as a consultant for Ryobi, developing lures with Bruce Vaughan who obtained them with a view to testing and, if they proved successful in UK waters, marketing

them through Ryobi. One batch was of 6in-long imitation rubber fish armed with one treble. Barrie had these with him on a bait-fishing trip when inclement weather had forced him beneath his brolly. At that point the gamekeeper arrived and laughed out loud at the rubber jigs. Half an hour later his laughter subsided as Barrie took six good pike from the swim without moving from his brolly and without winding in his two bait rods. Rubber lures took quite a while to catch on but now they are amongst the best lures in our bags.

Plugs

Some particular brands of plugs became very famous. We have already mentioned the Creek Chub range, but Abu's Hilo, with its easily-adjustable diving vane, and Shakespeare's Big S, were also deservedly well-known and widely used. Bomber baits, too, and Rapalas of course, together with the aforementioned, probably took up most of the room in the lure anglers tackle bag.

Many of these lures could be used on the troll as well as being cast from boat or bank. Charlie Bettell in his lure book singles out Kwik Fish, Lazy Ike, Beano, Tadpole and the Canadian Wiggly as trolling lures, but we used all of those very successfully from the banks as well, and many others on the troll.

A cautious approach is always needed when lure fishing, where possible keeping rushes between angler and water.
Photo: Barrie Rickards

Spoons

Many more spoons became available in the 1980s, such as the Landa range, with which both Barrie and Tim Cole helped and advised the manufacturers. In fact, the late Tim Cole became so successful with spoons that he abandoned use of plugs, especially those with several sets of trebles, and went for the easier to unhook spoons. He also argued that spoons were kinder on pike than multi-trebled hooks. In his last years almost all his lure fishing was with spoons, spinners and spinnerbaits, the exceptions being when surface-lure fishing, which he loved, and when using a minnow-style plug, usually small. We haven't so far mentioned the latter as they are not very different from other crankbaits. They are more elongate, slimmer, and have a very rapid wobble on retrieve. Rapala have long made a great range of minnowbaits including floating divers, deep divers and sinkers. Many of those are exceptionally useful for trolling. There is a gap, in our view, in the spoon market, for two things. One is for a serious wobbling spoon, which should have a low S-shaped profile. We have become too enthralled with the simple spoon shape such as the Norwich or the Vincent. The second is for a spoon full of holes, to create low-frequency vibrations. On occasions, our own do work better that the traditional.

Spinnerbaits

Pike lure enthusiasts have always used spinners, but perhaps they play second fiddle nowadays to plugs and spoons. The range available is huge. In the 1950s you could count the range in single figures, the best know being Ondex and Veltic bar spoons, and we have earlier on mentioned the Colorado and Kidney spoons. By the 1980s the range had increased tenfold, some firms, especially Mepps, making spinners of almost all kinds. To some extent today's pikers neglect them, although the ruse has not declined for trout, perch and salmon. Pike do prefer a small lure sometimes and when this happens a spinner may be as good as a tiny plug. There is one form of spinner available now, but not in the 1980s, which we will mention at this point merely for convenience. This is the 'electric' spinner. It produces a tiny electric current and occasionally will produce good bags of pike, Barrie getting several double-figure fish and a twenty-pounder on one occasion. The electric field cannot be detected by humans (Barrie put one in his mouth full of water!) but it can certainly be detected by pike and they home in on it.

There is one other aspect of lure fishing that hit us in the 1980s, and which certainly contributed to sustaining the lure-fishing boom. That subject is spinnerbaits. In this case we can attribute a little credit where perhaps it is due. The first person to mention those lures was, as far as we are aware, Fred J. Taylor – again! This was in the 1960s, when he described their use in weedy waters. However, because of the real explosion in bait-fishing techniques his wise words were ignored and the idea of using spinnerbaits did not catch on.

Nothing then happened until the 1980s when Bruce Vaughan, then developing Ryobi's lures, sent a box of spinnerbaits to Barrie for testing. They were such unlikely looking lures in Bruce's eyes that he sent them as a joke. They looked unlikely to Barrie too, but he dutifully tested them out – and caught a very large number of good pike, in a total of a few hours' fishing, from a whole range of waters. Bruce was a little taken aback, but went into action quickly with respect to marketing. The lure that Barrie had found the most successful was one with a copper blade and a chocolate and orange skirt, so Bruce imported large numbers of these and sold them under the title of Barrie's Buzzer. In just over a year, more than 10,000 were sold. The term 'buzzer' was just a little unfortunate, and resulted from the fact that the very first pack we received was labelled as such. Buzzers are, in fact, slightly different, slow-retrieve spinners that have a spinner head in-line with the tassel or skirt. Very quickly a huge range of spinnerbait types appeared, with varied blades, varied colours and varied sizes. Firms such as Pearce Lures made superb examples as well as bags to carry them in. They remain today one of the most successful and useful lures. Pike love them, and they can be fished at range, easily, and at any depth. Everybody accepts them nowadays as just another very good lure, but the origins in this country are exactly as we have described.

Influences from the USA

One thing you will have noticed, reading this chapter, is how many exotic names there are for our lures. Many of these names come from the USA and reflect not only their exuberance for lure fishing, but their marketing skills. It contrasts with the rather staid lure names of the 1950s and 1960s UK stables, but it also epitomizes a sea change in lure-fishing attitudes and approaches. Beginning with John Milford and all his friends, with TG Lures, with New World Lures, with Pearce Lures, we were dragged by the scruff of the neck into parity with the Americans who had led the field for a hundred years. Even now we are not quite there. Those of us who had been lure fishing quietly away, learning and adapting slowly, were quite happy to get involved in the enthusiasm and turmoil of the new lure fishing. Again, typifying this change is the fact that Charlie Bettell wrote his timely book (and also took over Barrie's column in *Coarse Fisherman*!). It is time now for another good lure book because the decade since Charlie Bettell has seen yet more changes. We'll come to this in due course.

Improved Tackle

At the moment, though, we'll do one of our digressions, because something we have been neglecting in this saga is the matter of tackle, including end tackle and peripheral tackle. About rods and reels it is not necessary to say a great deal. Most fixed spool and multiplier reels are quite excellent and a vast improvement on those available up to 1970. Two improvements have occurred that affect the lure angler in particular. One is that, just recently, manufacturers of fixed-spool reels have been cutting out the wobble that seemed for a while to affect the through handle, especially when the anti-reverse was engaged. Most reels are now left- or right-hand wind and the handle attachment bar goes through the body of the reel and out the other side. But, for several years, this bar was very rocky and could, in fact, jam. They seem to have cured this problem and it

certainly makes lure fishing with a fixed spool reel all the more pleasant. Malcolm's first ever lure-caught pike was taken with a Mitchell 324. He then used the 300 for many years.

The second improvement is the availability of left-hand-wind multipliers. Of course, these have always been available, but not in many ranges. Now most models have a left-hand-wind version.

Consider this: all right-handed anglers use a left-hand-wind fixed spool reel, keeping their stronger right arm/wrist holding the rod; but all right-handed multiplier users did, until recently, wind in with their *left* hand on the rod, and their right hand on the reel. Quite mad! Fred J. Taylor once tried to argue that it was something you got used to. This is quite true, but it does not make it right, or efficient. If you cast with your right hand on the rod, as the primary mover, then just as the rod drops to the horizontal position,

Barrie unhooking a pike taken on a jointed plug.
Photo: Barrie Rickards

so the reel handles drop comfortably *and immediately* to the fingers of the left hand. This has to be more efficient. Having used both approaches frequently, we are totally convinced we are correct about this. Fishing our recommended way is just more comfortable.

Anti-Kink Vanes

As with all pike fishing in the half century under analysis, keen lure anglers have effected a whole series of improvements away from the rod and reel. We mentioned earlier the fact that some lures, spinners in particular, cause line twist, or would do so if an anti-kink mechanism was not in use. Most anglers, ourselves included, spurned anti-kink vanes initially because they are an encumbrance on the end tackle, and a fiddle and they are against the long-instilled Walkerian principles of simplicity. Unfortunately, they are very necessary because one simply cannot cast well if the line is forever balling up in a bird's nest. The first anti-kink vanes an angler is likely to come across, because they are cheap, are plastic half-moon varieties with a swivel on one end and a link swivel on the other. These work quite well except that under real pressure from a strong current or a strongly vibrating lure, they do occasionally turn over, which can lead to line twist. We got around this by clipping a swanshot or two on the curved edge of the half moon, but Charlie Bettell came up with a better idea – a sphere of balsa glued to the half moon blade, one hemisphere on one side, one on the other. In either of these cases the anti-kink vane is seriously anti-kink.

There is one other anti-kink mechanism, which works well in our experience, and that is the Wye lead. In this the lead weight is an elongate half moon, and it hangs down from the line above the trace on the reel line, thus preventing any kind of spin. It is more expensive than the plastic variety but it works extremely well and comes in a variety of sizes. These leads have been around a very long time so cannot be claimed as an invention of the great modern pike anglers!

The problem with any anti-kink mechanism, partly aesthetic, is that the spinner and vane work against each other during the cast and the terminal tackle may wobble a bit in flight. It does not detract from the distance too much but it is not so pleasurable in use as a direct link to the lure. When plug fishing an anti-kink vane is unnecessary, of course, but the downside of this is that the lure fisherman may be reluctant to try a spinner, when perhaps he should.

Traces

Earlier in the book we mentioned how traces have improved from the early days when they were thick and black. It is possible that the pike don't really care at all because one of the best traces we have used for lure fishing is plastic-coated wire: and these are, surprise, surprise, thick and black. Wafer thin seven-strand wires are probably unsuitable for lure fishing because they really do seem to curl up at the least provocation, so something like QED, PDQ, or Alasticum is probably better, or the plastic-coated variety referred to. Length of trace is very important. In the past they were far too short, and anything less than 12in should not be used. If that's all you happen to have, then use two in tandem. Big pike will very often engulf totally quite large lures, such as Bulldawgs, and if the trace is say, 6in, then they can engulf that too.

Swivels

Swivels seem to cause anglers real headaches for some reason. Most modern swivels are satisfactory. Ken Whitehead spent years trying to convert Barrie to the joys of ball-bearing swivels but never really succeeded. In fact, ball-bearing swivels *are* probably better for lure fishing: in spinning for example, they assist the anti-kink vane (Malcolm has never used an anti-kink vane, he has had no problems with his swivels) and they are stronger than standard swivels, they are also bigger and more expensive, but we doubt if the sight of a large swivel worries the pike. The only change in modern times to swivels, which has seriously helped the pike angler, and the lure angler especially, has been the development of cross lock link swivels of various kinds. These are excellent for attaching lures and, unlike traditional safety pin style swivel, do not open up quite so easily.

The Gaff

We turn now to the lure angler on the bank. Like his bait-fishing counterpart, a lot of what the keen lure angler does is designed to facilitate ease of movement along the bank (or efficiency in the boat). In each case care of the pike is paramount. The angler will have a rod in one hand, a pack on his back, or over his shoulder. So far, so good. But what is in the other hand? A gaff? A landing net? Well, up to and including the 1960s it would have been a gaff, especially for the travelling lure angler. Richard Walker improved the design of the pike anglers gaff, so that the hook was V-shaped rather than rounded (a salmon angler's need) but it didn't catch on because pike anglers imbued by the carp anglers' zeal, were moving towards nets. Barrie used Walker's gaff in the 1950s, abandoned it, and began hand landing lure-caught pike, and then latterly turned to landing nets when his pike got a bit larger on lures.

Landing Nets

In the 1960s landing nets were still knotted which, perversely, was better for lure fishing than the later micromesh nets. This was because with the knotted landing-net material, treble hooks did not get inextricably tangled in the mesh. In micromesh netting, treble hooks with barbs really are difficult to unravel. One early landing net of Malcolm's had so many holes in it from cutting out hooks, that he once netted a pike of 18lb that somehow swam out of the net through one of the holes. He re-netted the pike and bought a new net. This led anglers to start using barbless hooks for lure fishing. In our view those really do not work. Far too many spiralling pike come adrift during playing. Microbarbs would be enough and the manufacturers are very slowly moving towards microbarbs. Even microbarbs, good though they are for safety and humanely hooking pike, are difficult to untangle from micromesh.

You'll now begin to appreciate a problem, or two here. The modern lure angler is being slow to grasp the nettle. Most continue with micromesh, with or without barbed hooks. Or they mistakenly think hand landing is the answer. Hand landing is dangerous, particularly when using large plugs. Youngsters should not be encouraged to do it, and the experienced should know better. We have hand landed a great many pike in our (combined) eighty years of piking and we repeat, hand landing is silly and can be dangerous.

Types of Mesh

There is an answer. Nets are now available that are not knotted, are not micromesh, and any hook can be extracted from them in seconds. We first obtained ours from Cabelas in Nebraska, but they are now widely available. They are a little harder on fish then micromesh, but certainly far better than the old knotted nets (which rarely did any damage anyway). If a pike spins in the net, as often happens, it doesn't matter much because upon unrolling the mesh you will find it quite easy to untangle the hooks and hence deal with the pike. The mesh size on these unknotted, non-micromesh nets is now decreasing to around half an inch, which is about correct. The early ones were over an inch mesh size, which is little too large and can result in split fins. Of course, if a pike is netted properly, allowing it to bag to the bottom of the net whilst still in the water, this problem more or less disappears anyway.

You could argue that the modern lure angler is a bit behind the times on these issues. More progress should have been made and even now only a small minority of lure anglers use the right nets. It's no good having a beautiful unhooking mat with you if you then spend an age getting to the fish before you are in a position to unhook it. Incidentally, the bankside lure angler does not normally need an unhooking mat, because there's usually plenty of grass around. Instead of carrying a rather large unhooking mat, we suggest you carry a small roll of bubble plastic. It does the job just as safely, is light and less bulky, and you can have a fresh piece every trip. It works on boats too!

Now we come to another thorny problem where the lure angler simply has not embraced modern developments. Most of our landing nets have evolved from the word of carp fishing, in a phrase, from the days of Richard Walker and his large triangular nets. There's nothing wrong with these for carp fishing, on the contrary, but lure fishermen who use them are being casual (their choice, and perfectly valid at that) or they haven't thought it through, or done much rough bank fishing. Triangular nets in undergrowth or in long grass, rushes or reeds, are a real pain, and anglers using them tend to wander the banks without them, relying on hand-landing. Triangular nets get the points stuck on whatever vegetation is around, and you end up struggling along the bank, not strolling in comfort. Some of them are far too big anyway. Barrie uses a 32- or 34in diameter round landing net frame with a big, baggy Cabelas net on it. When actually fishing the rim of the net is simply leant against the left thigh. When moving on to the next swim the left hand picks up the rim and the net is simply towed along. Because it is round it doesn't catch up on things and it is no trouble at all to carry. Until quite recently it was rather difficult to obtain a large round landing net frame, but they are increasingly coming onto the market, partly as a result of pressure from anglers like ourselves. Round landing net frames are also much better on boats, for the same reasons as above (not that there are many bushes on boats, but there are lots of projections of one kind or another). Just watch what fun we have when Malcolm's playing a near-24lb pike on Barrie's video ('Success with a Lure'). The frames can also be hung outside the boat, on the rowlocks or hole pins for example. Try that with a big carp net. And if you are still unconvinced by these arguments try a large pike, in large triangular landing net of micromesh material, on a boat, and you see what we are getting at. You'll stoop to hand landing under such circumstances and if you get yourself impaled then it's entirely your own fault.

Other Tackle for the Lure Angler

Since we moved on to discussing peripheral tackle for the lure angler we may have given you the impression that in lure fishing things are a little behind developments in bait fishing and in these respects it is true. The 'inventions' of the great modern lure anglers are only now beginning to have an effect in the trade. True, there are millions of good lures, with lots of good manufacturers, but good peripheral gear is not that easy to get.

We have not mentioned the matter of forceps as yet. In bait fishing forceps are used nowadays by most pikers, although we shall deal with unhooking and care of pike in detail in Chapter 9. Forceps are useful for the lure fishermen where small lures are in use, but when bigger trebles are involved pliers are better, giving a firmer grip on the hooks. They do not have to be particularly long-handled pliers because pike will usually be hooked in the jaws, but it pays to use sizeable, well-made pliers otherwise they are no better than forceps. Unhooking gloves are as useful to the lure angler as to the bait fisherman, perhaps more so in that the hooks are often larger and there are more of them. A small pair of bolt-cutter type pliers are also needed to cut up hooks if it becomes necessary.

Methods of Carrying Lures

We are now left with the question: what else is it necessary to carry? After all, lure fishing should be a mobile, lightweight pastime. We already have a rod in one hand and a (correct) landing net in the other. How does one, then, carry all those posh lure boxes? The answer is that one doesn't. These boxes are for use as a base store in the car boot, or for use on boats. You simply cannot carry, in any convenient way, a large plastic box for miles along the bank. So the lure angler does one of two things. One is wrong. One is right. The wrong way is to stuff a small number of lures in one pocket in a tobacco tin, (or modern plastic 'tin'). This is wrong because it restricts one's choice of lures, both as to size and variety. Old books often extol the virtues of travelling light. 'A few lures in the pocket …' is an oft-used phrase. It is used by half-hearted or inexperienced lure anglers or the incurably romantic. The number of circumstances is really few when you know fairly positively what lures you will need, certainly with pike fishing.

The correct way is to carry enough lures with you to give you a chance on colour, size and type. It is amazing just how often a particular lure works when the rest do not. It varies from day to day on one water, and extremely commonly as you move from water to water. So how do you carry thirty lures, which is the minimum we'd

Tackle stand of ET Lures, at the beginning of the lure-fishing boom, with, from the right, Chris Leibbrandt, John Milford and Steve Gould (with spinnerbait on head). Photo: Barrie Rickards

judge necessary to give you enough flexibility? There are two ways, one easy, one less so. The easy way is to get a half-size, lightweight plastic bucket, and drop all the day's lures into it. Do not, as some people do, hang the treble hooks around the rim of the bucket. It looks neat but it is dangerous. The hooks catch in your trousers and/or flesh, or what is worse, vegetation lifts them neatly and surreptitiously out of the bucket. No, just dump all the lures in the bottom of the bucket. When you need to change lure simply lift one of them at which stage *all* the lures will come out in a heap, hanging from the one lure. Try it – it's good fun. It is also very easy to then make a selection and quickly untangle the lure. It works.

A better, or aesthetically neater way, is to have a special lure bag. But this raises a related matter, which we'll deal with before going on to describe the ideal lure-angler's bag. This matter concerns exactly how much or what else one should carry on what, after all, is supposed to be a quiet stroll by the waterside. Well, your backpack needs a little food and drink, the latter being very important in summer lure-fishing sorties to avoid dehydration and tiredness from a long walk. For summer bank fishing it is advisable to add some warm or waterproof clothing: in winter you may well be wearing it from the off. And you'll need a camera,

hopefully, as well as some unhooking tools. So where's the room for thirty-plus lures? Easy …

What happens is that when you put the bag on the ground, and unzip it, the first thing that appears is the lure roll-up: unroll it and all the lures are visible, neatly arranged, and untangled. This feature is based upon the understanding that the average lure fisher will be changing his lure more often than he will be eating. When Barrie was on an outing with the late Tim Cole, such an assumption could be questionable, but *most* anglers eat less often than they change lures. So the lures come to hand easily. Behind them are the other bits of the day's gear; firstly unhooking tools in a roll of bubble plastic, then food, drink and camera. The whole lot then goes on your back leaving the two hands free for rod and net. There are very few of these bags around, because the tackle trade is slow to get its head round this one. Roach Tackle made and sold a few in the 1980s. Mepps International was keen, looked into it, but failed to produce after one of their advisers (clearly totally ignorant of lure fishing) reported negatively, and none of the other big manufacturers has really showed much interest. But this is typical of modern piking and inventiveness. The angler works out and designs what is needed, a (usually) small firm sets up and manufactures it, and finally a big firm belatedly copies the idea. The ideas do not as a rule come from the large sections of the trade, but rather are initially thought up and driven by the great modern pike anglers.

No doubt, in due course, you will have a suitable, customer-designed lure bag. For the present you can make your own, and that's fairly easy too.

Stinger Trebles

There is one aspect of peripheral/terminal tackle that we haven't yet discussed and that is the question of stinger trebles. Wagstaffe and Reynolds brought these in, we believe. They were spoon fishing in Ireland and noted that a considerable number of fish came short at the lure, just missing the rear treble time and again. We've all experienced this. So they strung an additional treble some 3–4in behind the normal rear treble, attached by stiff wire. The idea was either that the pike would snap at it or, if coming short to the main lure, would 'lean' on the trailing treble and hook itself. This worked, but it caused considerable controversy, being deemed unsporting and tantamount to foul hooking. We can see their point. Although there are arguments both ways a majority of pike anglers seemed to come out against the idea and it did not become widely adopted as a technique. However, a later modification did achieve widespread acclaim because there was no hint of foul hooking involved. This technique involved adding a stinger treble direct to a single hook on a lure such as a spinnerbait. A lot of spinnerbaits come fitted with a single hook – Barrie's Buzzer, for example, always had a single hook. It does not always get a good purchase on the pike, often because the hard clamp of a pike's jaw lays flat the single hook so that you are 'pull-Devil pull-Baker' with a fish that is not actually hooked but merely clamped down on it. As soon as it opens its mouth the hook comes free. The stinger treble is added to the single simply by running the eye of the treble on to the bend of the single and letting it hang there. You can readily see that it is not a foul-hooking rig at all, but it does ensure that if a pike clamps hard on the lure then at least one point will be in a position that makes

it difficult for a pike to shake free of. Those lure anglers keen on singles-only fishing would do well to ponder on this matter. The actual stinger treble is best attached by firstly slipping a collar of valve rubber over its eye and then pushing the point of the single hook simultaneously through the valve rubber and the eye, This ensures that the treble hook does not fall off the single hook but is easy to remove if you wish to fish the spinnerbait in a thick lily bed or through sunken trees. The late Colin Dyson put us on to this way of attaching the stinger treble, though whether or not he invented it we cannot be sure.

You can see now where we are going in this chapter. There is indeed a sea change in lure fishing going on, but it started at a later stage than the revolutions in bait fishing, and it took place more gradually. At this stage in the chapter we have, perhaps, reached the late 1980s, and it is clear that the modern lure angler has made major advances, possibly the greatest advances in several hundred years of lure fishing. But there is a way to go yet. The 1990s and early part of the twenty-first century saw yet greater advances not covered in any textbooks. Even Charlie Bettell's *The Art of Lure Fishing* is increasingly out of date. There is an increasing need for a *textbook* of lure fishing that will help the beginner and experienced alike. So, what happened in the 1990s?

Lure Fishing in the 1990s

Well, one of the real revolutions was the introduction of jerkbaits – and the ensuing controversy surrounding the use of jerkbaits. We have mentioned them briefly above, but jerkbait fishing *sensu stricto* reached this country from the USA in the 1980s. Barrie's first experience was when Malcolm gave him a small selection of Suick jerkbaits in June 1992.

The start of the jerkbait era in British pike fishing has its roots in the north-west of England. In the early 1990s Dave Scarff was making several jerkbaits for his own use. Malcolm, too, was aware of the lure-fishing scene in the USA, having taken the famous *In Fisherman* magazine since 1986. Malcolm writes in detail of his own part in this story in his own CV elsewhere in this book. His published reviews in *Pikelines*, August 1992 and in two *In Fisherman* fishing videos, one featuring jerkbaits, caused a mini sensation and lead to the formation by Malcolm and Dave Lumb of the Lure Angler's Society:

Al Lindner presents the muskie film and the opening shot says it all. Two anglers working plugs from a mist-shrouded boat, then a big muskie takes a plug near the boat and as you would expect all hell breaks loose. Al Lindner then takes us through the early big muskies that were caught with clips of film from 1971, showing fish to 69lb, all I might add were killed. It is all so different nowadays, catch-and-release first promoted by Muskie Inc. – a conservation society formed in 1967 by Gill Hamm – changed anglers' attitudes to killing muskies, and pike I might add, much the same as the P.A.C. has done here since 1977.

The best time for big muskies is early September when the first frosts cool the water. They use big plugs – 8in – long and retrieve very quickly, working the plugs erratically. They also appear to use heavy line of 20–30lb, which is no surprise as repeated casting with large lures must take its toll on lighter lines of 10–15lb. The power of the muskies is unbelievable so there is little point in taking chances and losing a 40lb plus fish.

All the fishing is done from the boat – which no British video has yet shown – and during the film many clips show fish to 30lb caught and lost, with clips of big muskies following the lures to the side of the boat then turning away at the last minute – not always a missed fish, they do a quick figure of eight and bang, the action begins. You just have to see it to believe it. All the fish are hand landed expertly, except one very big muskie, which is netted by the use of a folding cradle.

The film covers rivers, reservoirs and big lakes where you cannot see the land in the distance. Location as one would expect is discussed in depth, as is weather and water conditions in relationship to where and when to fish, covering all the calendar periods which range from summer to winter and are known as ice, pre spawn, spawn, post spawn, pre summer, summer peak, summer, post summer, turn over and cold water.

One thing is for sure. I intend to catch a muskie or two and have already started making plans for a holiday such is the impression this film left with me. I give it 10 out of 10 for entertainment and also for ability to illustrate how and where to catch muskies and more importantly, how very exciting lure fishing can be.

After the muskie film I thought *Fly Fishing for Pike* would be somewhat slower – just how wrong one can be! Larry Dahlberg does the commentary and the fishing, and was I impressed with this guy – a man after my own heart.

All the fishing on the film is done in shallow water, up to 4ft deep in the pre- and post-spawn periods. Larry states that fly fishing for pike in shallow water is probably the most fun you are likely to get from pike fishing. It is a method overlooked by most anglers and in certain times and situations it will catch pike more than any other methods. He uses floating lines with large 8in flies, which are very light indeed. He also shows you how to make these large flies and I fully intend not only to make some, but also to catch some good pike too.

He fully explains how you will need balanced tackle with these large flies, how to tie the Bimini Twist and Albright, special knots for fly fishing for pike. He catches fish to around 25lb on the film and it is absolutely unbelievable watching, as the pike follows and then grabs the fly with such speed and ferocity it seems almost unreal.

Compared with the muskie film, *Fly Fishing for Pike* is a different type of film, as one would expect – shallow water, very light tackle and flies, and at times Larry actually stalks the pike. For excitement and knowledge passed to the viewer I think it actually surpasses the muskie film, if that is possible.

Barrie Rickards and Geoff Latham gave them their support and in June of 1993 the Lure Angler's Society held their first fish-in at Esthwaite Water. Dave Scarff caught several fish to 26lb on his own jerkbaits. Malcolm too had a large bag of fish, 150lb plus, which included two doubles on the Suick jerkbait. These catches did not go unnoticed and very soon afterwards Dave Lumb, Nigel Grassby, Tony Martin and Mick Burnside were taking large bags of pike on Dave Scarff's and their own jerkbaits. Others like Dave Kelbrick very soon followed, and the rest, as they say, is piking history.

Concerns about Jerkbait Fishing

The controversy about jerkbait fishing is really an echo of the concerns raised by Tim Cole, which we mentioned above. Jerkbaits need not be large, but they often are, and the hooks are big. Like all hooks the barbs are too big. Added to that, the pike will often totally engulf a big lure, even one of 9in or so in length, and in doing so, two or three sets of trebles are in its jaws and have to be removed. Pikers have designed and carry cutters that will cut a stubborn treble to bits in no time but it still must be admitted that more damage is caused by big jerkbait hooks than by other lure hook rigs. Things could be improved dramatically if the hooks had microbarbs, but until that happens anglers can press down or file down the barbs. If this is done we think damage is negligible and probably no worse than when a pike engulfs a large perch as a meal. Once again, this exemplifies the angler's concern for the pike as well as reflecting on his innovation (the introduction of jerkbaits and his determination to improve on what has gone before). It does no harm at this point to emphasize what has been happening in this pike-fishing revolution. First there is the attempt to improve catch rates by a much better understanding of a pike's behaviour. Secondly, there is the inventive improvement of tackle to meet the objectives (usually taken up by firms at a later date). And finally, there is the honing of the tackle and approach so that the pike is well looked after. In one sense only there were changes in this philosophy, as the end of the last century drew near, but we shall deal with this later in the book.

Fishing from Boats

One of the big changes in the 1990s was the huge improvement in lure fishing for pike from boats.

As pike fishing on reservoirs became more readily available, anglers often went afloat for the first time. For those of us, such as the authors, who have boat fished for decades, many of the discoveries have been a revelation. Boat fishing, especially trolling, *was* going on back in the 1960s. For example, Wagstaffe and Reynolds both fished in Ireland and on the Norfolk Broads, either by trolling or casting from a stationary boat, the latter usually in Norfolk. Ray Webb also lure fished from boats in the same locales as Wagstaffe and Co. but also on rivers throughout the UK. Many anglers were lure fishing on Loch Lomond thanks to the inspiration of Richard Walker, Fred Buller and Bill Giles especially. Even at this stage of development some improvements had been made to the old trolling typical of Irish loughs. For example, many anglers used unhooking mats on the bottom boards, rod protection pads on the gunwales, outriggers as rod holders (to keep the butt of the rod from cluttering up the boat, and the lure itself a further 5–6ft away from the boat's line of travel) and the first echo sounders were in use (we both used a Seafarer, which still works!). Storage of lures on board was also improved. This had to be, because the modern troller was carrying far more and varied lures. Big plastic boxes were used as safe storage, tube systems were developed, and Barrie once toyed with use of carpet on the gunwales to which lures were attached in rows. (He gave that up when it proved too difficult to remove the trebles from the carpet!)

Both of us have done a great deal of boat fishing over the years and we own several small boats between us, but the modern pike angler has moved on from our own experiences with the most superlative custom-built craft, that is, built for anglers. Echo sounders are now very sophisticated, have side-scan facilities as well as vertical show, and colour displays which put to shame the old Seafarer: on the latter you can distinguish weed beds, thick mud, and fish shoals and that's about it apart from depth.

Boat Safety

More importantly, there have been many articles in recent years about safety in boats and about handling boats, especially anchoring. It is a good idea to look at where we were until around 1975–80 when boats and facilities began to improve. We have fished in Ireland in boats that were clinker-built and leaked all day long, needing repeated bailing. Barrie had a 17ft Shannon longboat, clinker-built, that didn't leak and it was a pleasure to use, if a heavy pleasure. It was extremely stable in rough weather. He would either troll on the outboard – the engine ran just a little too fast – or on the oars with the rod butt or butts secured beneath a foot bar: in rough weather read 'butt' in the singular! Water depth was learnt by experience, or, later, by using a Seafarer. The boat had no other angler refinements of any kind. Barrie's first (small) boat in the UK, was fitted out with padded gunwales, on which rods could be dropped safely, with on-off outriggers for rods, and, with a decent anchor, long rope, and a mud weight or two. Many pike-anglers' boats would be little better than this, but were increasingly of fibreglass rather than marine ply or wood. When Malcolm went to fish Loch Lomond he would always book the boat 'Robin' and can remember spending countless hours with a black bicycle cape over him to keep the rain and cold winds at bay.

Boat Equipment

Of course, you can still fish like this quite successfully if you are not boat fishing every week or travelling often from water to water, irrespective of likely weather conditions. So many of the modern pike angler's crafts have a small cabin; proper seats in the right places; safe oar attachments; good outboard transoms; an electric outboard for slow, controlled trolling; an echo sounder as good as TV; good, powerful outboards capable of running at a nice tick-over trolling speed; possibly bait wells (though this isn't necessary for lure fishing, it can be filled with lures!) and so on. The boat-fishing results of lure fishermen have increased strongly in recent years and at least part of this must be put down to better craft that can be easily transported, launched and winched out again: in short they are efficient and comfortable. We saw in the bait-fishing chapters just how this

leads to better piking. We'll deal with other aspects of boats in Chapter 8.

The 21st-Century Angler – Where Next?

The development of lure fishing in the last ten years has reached a peak that has probably never been seen before. It is true that lure sales, in 2005, began to decline somewhat, but this is hardly surprising given the huge numbers now out there in tackle bags, and the willingness of almost all commercial outlets to get on the bandwagon of lure sales. If there is a continued fall of sales then the lure anglers will benefit in the short term as lure prices fall, but it is difficult to know which way this one is going to break. There seems to be no decline in the number of lure fishermen, in fact the numbers seem to us to be growing steadily, especially now that it is widely realized that many more species than pike will fall to lures. So it could go either way. But in any event the approach to lure-fishing techniques and philosophy shows no signs of decline. As every month goes by we ourselves get new insights into tackle and techniques: to those of us lure fishing for pike in the 1950s and 1960s it is all very heady.

Earlier in this chapter we gave a run down of the lures available at the end of the 1980s and into the early 1990s. What is available in 2006? Which are the going lures? Is it possible to say what will happen next? At this stage we need to mention a few names. So far we have mentioned only a few anglers who were in at the start. Through the 1980s there were few pioneers except perhaps Gordon Burton – of whom more in Chapter 8 – but the new century did bring a breed of lure anglers who seemed to catch big. We are thinking of anglers like Derek MacDonald, Dave Lumb, Dave Kelbrick, Mick Brown, Tony Martin, Nigel Grassby, Mick Burnside and, more recently, Mark Ackerley and Eric Edwards, who have done very well at Blithfield. Mark likes his 'Squirrley Burt' Lures, and Dave Kelbrick also wrote superb articles questioning all aspects of lure fishing. Malcolm organized all the early Lure Angler's Society fishing at Esthwaite Water. He found it very hard to convince Dave Kelbrick that it would be worth the effort to attend the fish-in. Dave had done very little with lures till the Esthwaite 1993 bash. He wrote a splendid article on his day's fishing for the Lure Angler's Society magazine, *Lure Angler*, and is rightly one of the country's top lure anglers, working full time for The Fox Tackle Company. Those anglers in particular seemed to drag lure fishing up to American standards, and taught us so much about how to fish lures; how to choose a lure that would fish in a particular way; and how to go about a lure-fishing day and, most impressively, how to catch big pike on lures. The arrival of those anglers also coincided with the real boom in the full use of jerkbaits: they were contributors to it, and latterly they have contributed well to the use of rubber lures. It is true, as we explained earlier, that use of these began a long time go, but now they are *widely* used, and in a big range of styles and sizes. People now have some idea how to use them, how to modify them and how to fish them as jigs.

Some of the best lures currently around are quite large. We earlier mentioned the Bulldawg and it is a good lure to begin this part of the discussion with. When they first appeared in the UK the size of them took away the breath of some anglers, but they were extremely successful lures (even when trolling for zander, as we have found). Bulldawgs are made by Musky, and they do a similar Deep and Shallow Invader; Odyssey do the similar Pig-Tail. Not dissimilar, but entirely rubber or soft plastic are Zoota's Wagtails (rather different from the old salmon anglers wagtails, being up to 12in long); Twin Fins (up to 10in with *two* rubber tails like so many plastic lures); Storm soft plastics (a huge range from 4–8in long)… and so on, including a now phenomenal range of crankbaits (or floating or sinking divers) – and we haven't really said much about jerkbaits.

In looking though one recent lure catalogue, *Predator 8*, with a view to restocking our jerkbaits, we counted (excluding Fox's micro jerkbaits) around seventy different coloured, sized or shaped jerkbaits all more or less large. Add to that key jerkbait bodies that are similar, with a diving lip attached (which you can usually take

off in sections, and you get some idea that jerk-baiting has caught on.

Jerkbaits were developed in North America for fishing and it seems that the action, imparted more by the angler that the lure design, is one of a fish (that is, prey) with problems. By carefully using the rod to impart action to the lure the angler can get a variety of actions from one bait, but all are rather more erratic than the swimming style of an uninjured fish. Whether this is why the pike take them is perhaps another question, but it does look that way on present experience.

When people like Dave Scarf, Dave Lumb and Dave Kelbrick began to get success with big jerk-baits they realized that the rods that lure fishermen normally used were inadequate. In addition, there was considerable wear and tear on the lines, be they braid or monofil. So they designed special jerkbait rods that could be used with braid of 60–80lb BS. It is not necessary to have such strong lines in order to *catch* the fish, but it is necessary so that you can chuck big lures all day. The same applied to reels. We do not recommend fixed-spool reels for fishing large jerkbaits. Malcolm discussed this in detail with Dave Lumb many years ago. Line overlay was a serious problem when using a fixed-spool reel for large jerkbaits. Many jerkbait anglers use good multiplying reels for their jerkbait fishing, as we ourselves prefer to do. The multipliers are best in left-hand wind (for right-handed anglers) and here there is no doubt: if you are casting all day with powerful equipment it matters that everything is reliable, smooth and comfortable. It's crazy to change hands after casting and before reeling in.

The late Dave Scarf may not be a familiar name to today's lure anglers but he had considerable impact in the early 1990s. He began his lure fishing in Zimbabwe after black bass, using soft plastics, spinner baits, crankbaits and top water lures and continued this in the UK around Milton Keynes. He moved to the north-west where he convinced Dave Lumb and Malcolm that on occasions lures would outfish live- and deadbaits, clearly a persuasive character. Dave began making his own jerkbaits after watching American videos and later his own Fish Eagle Lures were promoted through the Lure

Angler's Society magazine. The most popular of Dave's lures were the Pig and the Dolphin, together with the Top Doctor surface stick bait – which accounted for nine 20lb pike in the two days of the second Lure Angler's Society fish-in in 1994. His lures were later taken up in the USA, becoming Odyssey Lures, and several outlets are now available around the world. Sadly Dave died in 1996.

Jerkbait fishing hit us big time in the late 1990s though it had been around some time as we said earlier. It has a big following and is an approach – a very successful approach – that has never before been seen in lure fishing in the UK.

We think the same can be said of the use of rubber baits and jigs. Thanks to the writings of Mick Brown and others, the jig lures have taken off well. People seem surprised, and most certainly they are pleased because it's an enjoyable art to learn. But they really shouldn't be surprised: Barrie and Ken Whitehead wrote about it back in 1976 in *Plugs and Plug Fishing*, having employed

the technique successfully in the 1960s. There is now a mind-bending range of rubber lures and jigs available in all sizes, shapes and colours. If lure anglers have discovered one thing in the last fifty years it is that one can never tell which colour shape or size is going to succeed on a particular water on a particular day. We have very few insights into this question, but we do realize that trial and error from a big choice of baits is the best way to proceed, and that too is good fun.

It is amusing to the old hands to see modern anglers slowly realizing that some lures are not easy to categorize. Because there are so many hybrids it's not easy to say whether something is a plug, or a spinner, or a fly, or a spoon. It was always so in the USA but only in the last half century has it been the case in the UK. In their 1976 lure book Ken Whitehead and Barrie figured a classification-cum-usage diagram and we include it here, modified, for the year 2005. It still works, even if the names have changed more than a little.

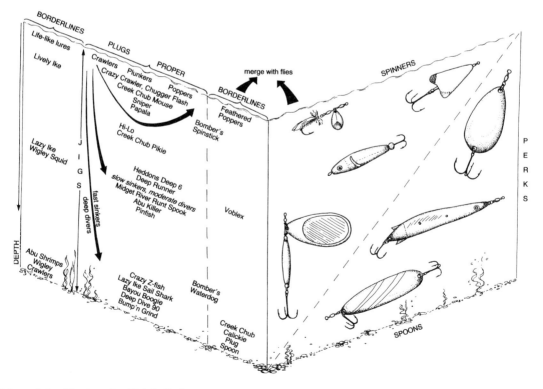

Natural classification of artificial pike lures.

5 FRED BULLER AND BILL GILES

It is appropriate that we devote a whole chapter, inadequate though that may be, to the subject of Fred Buller and Bill Giles. Although they are now regarded as the grand old men of pike angling (using that phrase in its most positive sense), it is also worth reminding ourselves that their contributions to an understanding of pike and to pike angling go back many decades.

Fred Buller

In the Foreword to Fred's seminal work, *Pike* (1971), Richard Walker wrote, 'In all my angling

Fred Buller, along with Bill Giles, regarded as one of the greatest pike anglers, and perhaps the best pike historian. Photo: Fred Buller

career I have known of no one whose enthusiasm for catching and learning about a particular species of fish equals that of Fred Buller for pike'. It is of interest that a man of whom many would have declared the same obsession with carp wrote that!

The book, *Pike*, was and is one of the great books on pike angling. The contents of it provide a direct link between the anglers and styles we dealt with in Chapter One and the pike-angling scenarios up to 1970. What one might term the *new* piking, which we describe in Chapter Two and epitomized in *Fishing for Big Pike* (1971), was being established in the 1960s and is only partly covered in *Pike*. That apart, it is a book of enormous breadth and scholarship. Part I begins with accounts of 'Great Pike' such as John Garvon's record, or the Whittlesea Mere pike, and this section is a prelude, really, to his other seminal book, *The Doomsday Book of Mammoth Pike* (1970), which lists all the known pike weighing 35lb or more. In fact, as well as listing them, it gives all known details of capture, weighing and location in a very scholarly yet highly readable fashion.

We would argue that *Pike* brought us right up to date in 1971 with the whole subject of pike angling: its myths, its lore, the techniques and, especially, the biology and way of life of the pike. All techniques, old and new, sporting and unsporting, were thoroughly covered and illustrated. It is a quite astonishing compendium of myth, history and fact, and it provided considerable encouragement to the pikers of the day. It is also a substantial tome that thumps healthily on to the desk.

The *Doomsday Book of Mammoth Pike* has all these qualities and, more than *Pike* perhaps, it has *inspired* pike anglers as no book has done before or since. You may or may not believe the weights of all the fish recorded, and we are sure Fred himself did not, but there is no escaping the shear scope of the work and the terrific level of scholarship achieved in setting before us the accounts of capture of these enormous fish: the term 'mammoth pike' seems reasonable! What we feel makes the book rather special is that the accounts are not dry-as-dust factual, but often show pictures of the water, or actually swims in question, and they include anecdotes surrounding the captures. It has occurred to us many times that the capture of unusually large fish is so rare an event that almost always there is something odd about the day, or about the capture itself. When Barrie caught two thirty-pounders in one day he would not have done so had he not got bogged down in a snowstorm in the middle of a ploughed field; had that not happened he

would have fished a different swim entirely. That kind of thing seems so often the case, and Fred documents every last scrap of information, and waves in front of the reader every possible implication. It is good that Neville Fickling has updated Fred's work in a recent (2004) book, *Mammoth Pike*, so the most successful pike angler in history follows the most accomplished pike-angling historian. It seems fitting.

As we write this we understand that Fred Buller has another tome in preparation that includes these spectacular European captures of pike that to some extent dwarf captures in the UK. More recently, Fred has published a smaller yet quite splendid book, *Great Pike Stories* (2003). These are good stories taken from a variety of sources, ancient and modern, the aim being to provide a good fireside read rather than a compendium of big pike, and he succeeds in delighting, amusing and enraging the reader.

Fred Buller lure fishing in rough country.
Photo: Fred Buller

In a way, we should have been forewarned of this dramatic outpouring of major works on pike by Fred Buller, because the equally classic work he did with Hugh Falkus, *Rigs and Tackles* (1967), is not only of similar great breadth, but contains quite a lot on pike rigs and tackles. And, of course, they also did a monumental work, *Freshwater Fishing* (1975). You could argue that it is not only ironic, but also perhaps unjust, that a failed knot on Loch Lomond deprived Fred Buller of what would probably have been his biggest ever pike. In the same foreword to which we referred above, Dick Walker wrote, 'But for an unreliable knot, Fred Buller would now hold the world record for *Esox lucius*. This I know, because I saw the immense fish he hooked . . . at a distance of not more than six feet'. Dick does not mention the weight of the fish at that point but elsewhere in print he states that the fish was over 50lb. Fred Buller in *Pike*, page 212, says that, initially,

Walker went for 40 or 45lb. In private letters, however, he goes further, averring that the fish could not have been less than 60lb. One of Dick Walker's purposes in highlighting this particular loss was to persuade pike anglers to head for Loch Lomond to try to break the British record. However, we have no doubts that he genuinely believed the fish to weigh so much because we have talked with him about it. Barrie has never been quite convinced that Dick was in a good position to make a good judgement of the size of the fish: fish of 30lb or more look very, very large if you are sitting down and they appear at the surface only a few feet away! Malcolm thinks between 35 and 40lb was more likely. And was Dick Walker a good judge of pike weights anyway? We shall never know, but would it not have been splendid had we been able to have as a feature of this chapter, Fred Buller, record holder? It would have been appropriate, in so many ways.

Fred Buller afloat on Loch Lomond, scene of his epic battle with a giant pike; and the venue that he persuaded many pike anglers to try. Photo: Fred Buller.

Bill Giles

Bill Giles is a different kind of person in some respects, but has the same dignity of presence and inestimable good manners of Fred Buller. They are two of the real gentlemen of angling. Bill has written chapters in books, including a long appendix in Fred's book, *Pike*, and a number of articles for magazines, but he has written no books and tends to shun the limelight only rarely attending meetings, even as a younger man. He fishes. Of the older generation, he probably fishes more than anybody. He wrote to us on 2 October 2005, just after he got back from a trip to Canada where he had a trout on his last trip with his great grandson. Bill is 92 as we write, has three great, great grandchildren and seventeen great grandchildren. If just some of them take after him, we hope some of *them* become pike fishermen. We dealt with Bill's definitive role in the early development of deadbait fishing (Chapter 2). Just how effective he was can be gleaned from his lifetime's results: 66 pike over 20lb, best fish (1987) being 31½lb and 31lb (possibly the same fish, according to him, from Ranworth Inner Broad). It's worth remembering that Bill fished with methods from the old days, yet his skill and innovation resulted in more 20lb pike at that time than most anglers, including the legendary Ray Webb. Barrie fished with Bill on many occasions in the Fens, and can attest to his real generosity of spirit. He was always pleased to pass on tips and to explain his thinking as regards tackle and techniques, and it is by word of mouth rather than by publications that Bill Giles has advanced piking. It is fortunate that so many experienced pikers knew him and have fished with him and so are fully aware of where the help came from. For example, when *Angling Times* published the discoveries of Fred J. Taylor on deadbaiting, several of us already knew of Bill's progress in the Norfolk Broads: that he and Reg Sandys had independently of Fred J. re-invented the technique. Bill was also involved in the early exploration of Loch Lomond, fishing there with Fred Buller, Dick Walker and others and, indeed, catching pike to 24½lb. Whether or not

he believed the stories of 50lb-plus pike in Loch Lomond we know not, and have not pressed him, but in the meeting of pikers held in Milton, Cambridgeshire, Bill Giles seemed to have his feet firmly on the ground offered by the Fens and the Norfolk Broads.

At a time when most anglers used the pike rod as a second rod or, as Ray Webb and others were beginning to do, used two rods, Bill used four! The butts of all four rods were within a yard of where he sat and all had deadbaits on them. These were cast at different distances and angles, and might have different baits on them. He argued that dead-baiting could be a waiting game, so he sat there learning French from the radio, and discovered that four deadbaits in one swim was as good as groundbaiting. On getting a run on one rod he would drop the tips of the other three into the water, so that the line, already half sunk, sank fully, thus avoiding tangles. He had few tangles and plenty of fish. No one could accuse him of fishing unattended rods and, because he always ledgered the baits, you could not tell he was on the water until you tripped over him. In that way he was able to observe a lot of wildlife! In that simple sketch you can see how far ahead of the game he was in the late 1950s: ledgering deadbaits (unheard of); four rods (unheard of); groundbaiting for pike (in its early stages only); fishing at dawn (just published, though decried!).

If you look at his chapter in Fred Buller's *Pike* (1971), the same year incidentally as Webb and Rickards' *Fishing for Big Pike*, Bill gives a series of notes based upon his piking on the Norfolk Broads. The first thing he does is draw attention to the fact that big pike like a big food item, his first big pike of 1950, at 25½lb, had a 2lb bream inside it. This fish was set up, again a sign of the times. Both Fred Buller and Bill have drawn attention to the fact that pike were viewed differently before the late 1950s. Bill and Reg (Sandys) concluded that for big pike, herrings, mackerel and large dead roach are far better than livebaits.

This does not equate with Dennis Pye's success in the Norfolk Broads, of course, but it was the beginning of thinking that swayed many for a long time, not least Richard Walker.

*Bill Giles with another
big Norfolk pike.
Photo: Bill Giles*

Bill Giles with a 30lb pike from Norfolk. Photo: Bill Giles

Bill was one of the very few anglers to put great weight on noise when piking: lack of it is a distinct advantage. He points to the fact that many anglers start up their outboard motors even to move swim by a hundred yards or so. This makes no sense at all. Big fish can be caught very close to where the piker is sitting, but not if he is easily visible, noisy, or stamping about in hobnailed boots. Pike may not be crafty, but they *are* sensitive to their environment.

One point Bill makes is that he's never seen a waterfowl pulled under by pike. If someone who spends so much time on the water has never seen this, how come everybody else *has*? We liked his honest observation, which is more than one can say for some other observations, which are, in fact, merely folklore. Malcolm has seen it

and once removed a small duck from a pike's mouth. On both occasions the water in question was a shallow drain.

In the same chapter Bill also came out against another element of mythology, namely the need to allow a taking pike to have a second run. Very few agreed with him at the time, even Fred J. Taylor, but everyone does today. Bill also comes out against the use of the gaff, preferring a circular net (although he used to bend it to give a width of 28in!). The whole chapter was a breath of fresh air for pikers of the day and it beautifully complemented Fred Buller's book, which brought everyone up to date on all manner of piking matters. Bill's chapter pointed to the future and most of this book covers what followed thereafter.

6 BIG CATCHES

Ray Webb and Barrie Rickards in 1965 with part of a large catch including twenty-pounders. Photo: Barrie Rickards

Big catches of pike have always taken place, but it is our contention that not only are more big fish caught these days by more people, but that large catches of pike are more common too. There are many big catches recorded from before the 1960s and it is not our intention to belittle them in any way – often they were taken without the advantages of modern tackle and know-how and were the more creditable for that. We recall that not so long before Ray Webb 'cracked' Hornsea Mere in East Yorkshire, Ernest Merritt had recorded a catch of fifty pike on lure in one day, whilst Eric Allen took a trio of very large pike from the same water. These catches caused a sensation at the time and became embedded in our national consciousness as pike anglers of the day. Yet since this, Barrie has exceeded such catches himself and on another occasion shared 102 pike in two days with

two colleagues. Day catches of 100lb and 200lb to one angler are not uncommon today, but we venture to suggest *were* uncommon prior to the 1960s. The Norfolk Broads and the Irish loughs at intervals produced some huge catches but not as frequently as they have in recent years.

Increased Catches

There are lots of reasons for this, but amongst them are the facts that tackle is better, piking knowledge is greater, the amount of time fished is greater, and more people are doing it. There are also more pike waters with big pike in them. This in itself has several causes. Firstly, the pike is more cosseted than at any time in the past. Secondly, there have been no serious freeze-ups since 1963, and hence no serious winterkill. And there are far more waters than in the past – gravel pits and trout reservoirs in particular. Finally, there are more skilful anglers around: specialization has brought knowledge and ability, albeit in a narrow field, considering angling as a whole.

The increase in individual bags also related to matters we have discussed earlier in the book. It is to do with efficiency. Unhooking efficiency we discuss in Chapter 9 specifically, but overall, piking efficiency means that the pike angler is fishing well more regularly than in the past. Landing and unhooking efficiency means fish are returned to the water more quickly and hence there is a chance of another fish. When we think back to our early days the capture of *any* pike was quite an event and the whole capture and return certainly did take longer – and there were often quite a few spectators to view the dreaded fish, which didn't speed things up, especially if some of them wanted to kill it.

Changing Attitudes in Today's Pikers

Through the 1960s and 1970s an increasing number of big pike were caught – forgetting about the big bags for the moment. Even so, the number of 30lb fish in a season might number five or so. Today that number is caught in a week, quite often. And remember, today, not everyone reports these big pike because they hope to catch another one, or the same one. There is no doubt at all that pike angling has improved in the last fifty years. In consequence, the number of pike anglers has increased. How far can things go? In a recent article in *Pike and Predators*, Peter Waller of Norfolk, a self-confessed pessimist, argued that in the last fifty years, through which he had pike fished, he had probably seen the all-time acme of pike fishing: that in all probability it would decline from here on in. His point is that there are too many pikers now, and too many of them are in the numbers game, seeking results above all else. If this is

Jim Housden with a 34lb fish. Photo: Jim Housden

Jim Housden with a 28½lb pike.   Photo: Jim Housden

true then all the good work over half a century by a lot of people will have been wasted, in the long term. Malcolm thinks that it is not so much the numbers game, but the more selfish attitudes of a very small number of pike anglers: some are high profile and their actions put the future of pike fishing on some very good waters at great risk. We have all bent the rules to some degree over the years, but for some, the attitude is 'I do not give a damn' for others or for pike fishing in general. We fear it will always be.

There is, as yet, no indication that Malcolm is correct, and piking catches continue to improve. There is a cyclical effect, of course, with respect to particular waters. Barrie began fishing a water that had been 'fished out' ten years ago, and took a considerable number of twenty-pounders from it. He kept quiet. New waters come on tap too, but if waters can be fished out – and we discuss this further in Chapter 9 – then Peter has a serious point to make in that it is anglers who are the cause, not nature. Nature also operates cyclically too, of course, and we would not wish to deny that.

Is it necessary to take a big bag of pike? Well, it is certain that most anglers would like to, because the complete hectic nature of such a day brings its own rewards, which stay in the memory. But as one gets older it is the cracking of a water that really counts, along with the company you keep, and the occasional big fish. One thing we do not do nowadays is keep a big bag of pike in keepnets or keep sacks, although we have illustrated a couple of such catches just to give some idea as to how it was considered quite normal at one time. Barrie's best catch in one day, in terms of numbers, was over fifty, and several times has had over thirty, his second best catch numerically being thirty-eight in one afternoon. All these fish were returned quickly to the water, with a few pictures having been taken.

Increased Choice of Angling Techniques and Equipment

There is one factor we haven't mentioned so far in this claim of increased captures and that is the flexibility of the modern angler, which we established in Chapters 2 and 3. Anglers are not simply prepared to do one thing – lure fish or bait fish. They are now physically and mentally equipped to do anything that is necessary, switching from deadbait to lure or vice versa, either for a very good reason or merely just to try something different. At about the time the piking revolution got under way it was much more common to find anglers operating only one method, all of the time. As we have said elsewhere, even Neville Fickling has taken up lure fishing.

Some of the most amazing captures and bags have been made by some of our very famous, deservedly famous anglers. Peruse Neville Fickling's 'Big Pike' list and you will see Eddie Turner and Jim Housden who, with others, had rather spectacular catches of thirty-pounders from an Essex water. We perhaps need to distinguish the capture of an individual big fish, which can happen to anyone, anywhere to some extent, and the capture of large bags of fish or catches of large pike occurring frequently to one angler or a group of anglers. For example, in the 1960s the Cambridgeshire Pike Anglers repeatedly caught very large bags of fish, with a considerable number of 20lb-plus fish. Bags of 100lb, or even 200lb to one individual in a day, were not uncommon. In all probability, this had never been achieved before in piking, not even on the Norfolk Broads, not on a week-by-week basis at any rate.

Changing Patterns of Angling

This pattern of post-1950s success has been maintained and improved upon, as exemplified by the Eddie Turner and Jim Housden catches referred to. We do not intend to go through all the major catches since the 1950s, but would make the point that whereas such catches though the 1960s and 1970s were made by relatively few individuals, they have since then been made by many more anglers. The first,

Jim Housden with a 28¼lb pike. Photo: Jim Housden

relatively small group were among the pioneers of modern piking, and we deal with them in the next chapter. The second group is more difficult to define and account for, but we discuss them in Chapter 11. Of course, the one group merges into the other, as you shall see.

Where to Fish

Some of the big catches *are* worth a mention in emphasis of our points. For example, whilst the Cambridgeshire Pike Anglers were doing so well in Fenland, Martin Gay and others were succeeding with mammoth catches on Abberton Reservoir. Abberton is still famous and we have fished there ourselves, but when Martin Gay fished the water he had access to some hotspots not subsequently available to anglers, and he made huge catches with many big fish.

Many pikers have come from Sheffield and Derek Gibson is one of them. Now sixty-two, he is becoming an old stager, and one who has done his administrative stint for the Lure Angler's Society just like many other successful pikers. For a long time he was very cagey about his catches, which may not be a bad thing if you want to protect your piking, as we have argued elsewhere in this book. Derek was into wobbled deadbaiting in the 1960s, taking pike to 29lb from Lincolnshire. As did so many at the time, he used single-strand Alasticum, which was far from ideal for any form of casting and recasting. Fishing with Chas Taylor on the South Forty Foot they took 190 doubles, mostly on spoons and wobbled baits, during the winter of 1970/71. He also took large numbers of big pike, including seven twenty-pounders, from the River Hull in 1976–79. After that they moved on to Sheffield reservoirs taking their first 20lb fish in 1987, and subsequently huge numbers of big pike, over 200 twenty-pounders and thirteen thirty-pounders to 35½lb. Most of these fish fell to lures or wobbled deadbaits. Derek's greatest number of twenties in a season is twenty-six, two more than Dennis Pye's best season. It is an astonishing record by any standards.

If a particular Ardingly event triggered the lure-fishing revolution in Charlie Bettell's mind (Chapter 4) then Llandegfedd probably focused the minds of the big fish/big catch fraternity. A good example, perhaps the best, was Steve Gould's capture on lure of five twenty-pounders in one day, including large fish. The excitement in the angling world could be felt at any meeting you attended at that time. At a later stage Blithfield Reservoir had a similar effect on anglers, although in that instance (and Blithfield is still with us!) we are, as a rule, talking big fish rather than big catches.

The Norfolk Broads

Another example concerns the Norfolk Broads. Catches have always been good there, and the 1960s saw Hancock's 40lb fish, but since then

Bob Forshaw with a thirty-pounder from Loch Lomond. Photo: Malcolm Bannister

there have been several more such fish, other huge fish, and some terrific piking results which overshadowed – it is not really overstating the case – the historically important catches of the past. And the anglers were? Well, Neville Fickling, Derrick Amies, John Watson, Martin Page, Vic Bellars, David Batten, Steve Harper, Charlie Bettell, Dave Plummer, Colin Dyson, Bill Giles and Reg Sandys. Notice that all these pikers are thinkers, are pioneers, have contributed enormously to the sport and most of them became professionals in some manner or another. John Watson became the first ever pike-angling guide, and successful at that too, as well as being a tackle-trade consultant. Charlie Bettell did the same, concentrating on lure fishing. Malcolm too, became a winter pike-angling guide, the first in the north-west. However, while he could demonstrate at the water's edge how to fish and what tackle to use, he found that

in the Southport area he could not guarantee to put a pike on the bank. The local drains were and still are often unfishable due to heavy pumping. Not ideal fishing conditions and it is by catching and handling pike that the newcomer to our sport learns quickest. He remembers a prearranged trip to the Lake District on Rydall Water. This young man had booked well in advance and needless to say, the weather was appalling with very heavy rain which resulted in Rydal rising 3ft whilst they fished. They caught three pike each, which was a good result considering the conditions. Following that day he decided reluctantly that he could not give value for money living where he did. Neville is in the tackle trade. Vic Bellars and Martyn founded the highly successful Marvic Company manufacturing items that the big firms did not (then) want to touch. There seems to be a natural progression in these things: success in piking seems to

Barrie Rickards with two twenty-pounders and two big doubles, all on paternostered tackle, in days when keepnets were used to hold a bag of fish. Photo: Barrie Rickards

lead to a closer overall involvement in the sport. And many of them contributed in an unselfish manner to clubs, being officials and representatives of one kind or another. But they all caught big pike and big bags of pike and, for the most part, still do!

The Republic of Ireland

We have mentioned elsewhere that large catches were made in Ireland, especially by the Northern Irish Pike Society, but David Overy and friends in the Republic should also be mentioned. These anglers really did take Irish piking to a new level. And it is worth recounting also that the western Irish lakes played a part, despite the dismal record of pike slaughtering that has and still does take place there. In the 1960s Fred Wagstaffe and Bob Reynolds raised the stakes quite a bit, deliberately targeting pike rather than game fish with pike as an also ran. But others took matters to a higher level still in later years, notably Neville Fickling with his guided safaris to the western Irish lakes. Some very big fish and very big catches were made, again rather more consistently than in the past. Who is to say what might have been had the Irish authorities not continued their ill thought-out policy of pike extermination. Certainly, Ireland has fallen in the public conception of a piking venue. Why go to Ireland to fish for fish that may not be there, when you can go to Loch Lomond, the Broads, Blithfield or the Lake District or, indeed, get better piking in big English gravel pits?

The Lake District

That brings us to the Lake District, and its several big pike waters. Windermere, the biggest of these lakes, has a long history to do with pike and pike fishing and Fred Buller worked there at one time at the freshwater Biological Station at Wray Castle, studying perch populations among other duties. It is one of life's coincidences that Barrie mapped the rocks around Wray Castle as well as fishing the lake in the 1970s.

In the 1970s to the early 1980s the Lake District was not on the pike angler's route map. Books by Fred Buller and Jim Gibbinson had shown large catches of pike from Loch Lomond, whilst Barrie Rickards and Ray Webb's book, *Fishing for Big Pike* (1971), illustrated what splendid fishing the Fenland drains offered. So it was to these venues that the new breed of pike anglers like Malcolm, John Watson and Gordon and Barry Burton made their early forays. There was a large amount of travelling involved to both venues.

In 1978 on a holiday in the Lake District, Malcolm stopped at a lay-by next to Bassenthwaite Lake. Walking down to the water's edge near a shallow bay, an angler was sitting on his box, pike fishing. His one and only rod had several floats attached and he was fishing mackerel sections at 3ft deep in around 7ft of water. While Malcolm watched this spectacle the piker had several runs from some large pike that resulted in a tug-of-war, for that's what it was, which was won by the pike every time, mostly by tail walking and throwing the bait. Needless to say he was to revisit that particular area many times over the following years and it accounted for his Bassenthwaite personal best pike of 24lb 4oz.

Around the same time Pete Hesketh and Dave Lumb also started to visit Bassenthwaite. Malcolm remembers vividly being asked by another well-known Southport pike angler why we were bothering to fish Bassenthwaite Lake as Slim Baxter (of Lomond 34lb-pike fame) and Chris Bowman, who both lived locally, had allegedly caught nearly every pike in the water and never had a twenty. We took no notice of this advice and over the years that water was very kind to all three of us.

We fished it quietly with a lot of success, until someone blew the water to *Angling Times*. Malcolm details all his early Lake District fishing in his book, *Tales from a Pike Angler's Diary* (1993).

Bassenthwaite has produced several 30lb pike over the years but has gone off the boil so to speak, proving that even a large water can get overfished. Malcolm moved on to fish Derwent Water for several years (where pike are removed by netting). He caught lots of doubles from there, his best day being two at 18lb and a 14lb. The removal by netting is probably the reason why so few twenties are caught there. Windermere too is netted, but such is its expanse that it still produces a great number of pike between 20lb and 25lb. Thirty-pound fish are caught but on such a large water they are harder to find. Malcolm's first ever serious trip to Windermere boat fishing resulted in four twenties in his boat, all between 23 and 25lb; two each to himself and Steve Ball, his fishing partner on that day. Thirlmere, Rydal and Grassmere have, and still do, produce pike of over 20lb, whilst Esthwaite Water (a trout water) has been well documented as regards to its pike potential. Malcolm took his first 30lb pike (30lb 8oz) in January 1992 and in June 1994 on a gold Lucky Strike Lizard spoon he had his second thirty at 30lb 6oz. This fish and a 21½lb were caught in consecutive casts at a Lure Angler's Society fish-in.

The Lake District is a National Park, so one is fishing in glorious surroundings, a fact that helped Malcolm and other pikers to concentrate on these waters.

Any of these lakes could throw up a real surprise, such as the 38lb 4oz Coniston Water pike caught by Jason Gibson on 13 February 2004.

Angling pressure is making its mark on even these very large waters, but when the pike are on the feed one can catch very large bags, including a few twenties to boot.

Essex
Ardleigh Reservoir in Essex also hit the headlines, again for big fish rather than big bags of fish. Several session anglers and small groups of anglers were involved. Martin Gay was involved at a very early stage, knowing the then manager as he did, but the group that we think really epitomized the success there was Bill Palmer and friends. Bill is one of the grand old gentlemen of pike angling, one of the most successful too, and stands alongside Bill Giles and Fred Buller in his achievements and contributions, not least in his superb autobiography, *Dimples to Wrinkles* (1997, now updated). His catches have not only been on Ardleigh but on many other waters including big ones such as Abberton. Perhaps we should have mentioned Bill Palmer in the *next* chapter, but his roots go back to the very beginnings of the piking revolution. A bit more writing wouldn't come amiss from the legendary

Derek Gibson with one of his many giant pike from a northern reservoir, 30½lb, 1991. Photo: Derek Gibson

Palmer. Malcolm considers Bill's book one of the best of modern times, and just wishes he had as many good waters on his doorstep, so to speak, as Bill has.

We have ourselves often been involved in big catches of pike and in order to illustrate just how special and emotive these catches are, the following three accounts are taken from some of Barrie's most enjoyable results, the first being published in *Coarse Angler* (March 1990); the second with David Hall's permission (David Hall's *Coarse Fishing*, October 1988) and the last, with permission of the *Sheffield Star*, was first published on 27 March 2000.

Foggy, Foggy Dew

I'd been teaching most of Saturday morning, but as it was a cold and foggy December day I hadn't really begrudged giving up my day's fishing. Unlike most Universities, Cambridge works Saturdays and all public holidays which, from my point of view, is simply an invitation to take time off in lieu when other commitments allow! So I get in the odd mid-week angling trip now and again. This particular Saturday marked the end of a week of quite sharp frosts, and a lot of waters were frozen or partially so. Added to that several days had been foggy, not lifting all day. As I walked back to Emmanuel College, after my Departmental teaching had ended, it would have been about lunchtime, and I couldn't help noticing that it was a degree or two warmer – still very foggy, but decidedly milder. So I called into the office where there is a barometer graph print-out permanently set up, to see what might be in store. The graph was still rising: it had started doing so from a deep trough, some four or so days previously though this would not have helped me as the waters were frozen. Now it had reached the heady heights of 1035mb and was climbing even more steeply.

I was interested now! The next call was Emmanuel College pond, full of big carp. But what was interesting here was not the fact that the carp were cruising freely, but the fact that you could see them doing so. The ice had almost gone during the course of half a day. There is a stream flow through the pond – a diversion from the Cam called Hobson's Conduit (of Hobson's Choice fame) – and this no doubt had helped to free the water of ice. But the pike water I had in mind was a river, and it might be thawing quickly. To be honest I didn't really think so, but it was possible – I'd go look!

I don't need more than half an excuse to go fishing, and this *was* only half an excuse. I defended my decision by saying to myself that I'd go in my working clothes, the idea being just to see if the water would be clear for the Sunday. How we seek to kid ourselves!

The journey depressed me because there wasn't the slightest let up in the fog and my hopes dwindled as I parked in the farmer's yard. By now it was 1.30pm; but, undeniably, as I got out of the car, the air was mild and still. The river, as I broached the bank quickly, was totally free of ice. Birds were paddling and clucking with enthusiasm as they always do after a thaw. Back to the car... Here I pulled on over-trousers over my ordinary trousers, and a fishing coat over my tweed working jacket. And I just happened to have my waders, spinning rods, etc.!

The first ten minutes or so of spinning produced no takes, but it was good to be out again. It was now 1.45pm. I made a decision then which led to an amazing series of events. I did hesitate, because with the fog down to 50-yards visibility, one could hardly look along the river and receive inspiration from anywhere! But I decided to walk a mile or so downstream and try a section I hadn't been to for a long while. The walk got me nicely warm because milder or not, it was impossible to avoid the dampness of the fog, or keep spinning water off your fingers: although I had my winter spinning gloves on the damp would eventually penetrate under these conditions.

The river looked no different, except that there were a few more trees. The colour was superb for lures, being just off clear, and there was plenty of water, with a reasonable flow. I changed from a buzzer to one of Simon Pearce's Lucky Strike Lizard spoons, in silver and copper. To his amusement I always buy him out of these at the P.A.C. one-day conferences, but with ample justification to the tune of several 20lb pike on them in the last couple of years. I also carried what is turning out to be a magnificent team of spoons from Tony Perrin's Pikko stable: especially I had a combo-killer in perch and gold colouring, and some of his splendid pike imitations complete with bars and spots.

I started with the Lizard, flicking it downstream and across so that it fell close to an overhanging bush. I counted it down until it hit the bottom – five seconds, so about 5ft deep. The retrieve, after a flick to set it rocking, had gone perhaps ten feet or so when the rod tip dragged round slowly and heavily. I didn't feel anything in particular, but struck as I always do when in doubt: my strike resulted in a pike about 8lb coming completely airborne! The fish went berserk, with several leaps, and spiralling runs, headshaking, and several charges across the surface. When I finally netted it, it weighed 9lb. And the 6in spoon had been completely engulfed on the take. They do this when they chase them from behind, so I reckoned the fish had come out from under the overhanging tree on the far bank.

Composure recovered I tidied up the mess at my feet, and rearranged things a little so that my forceps were clipped to my unhooking glove which was tucked firmly into a pocket – a pull on the forceps would release them for quick use. I'd already removed my spinning gloves during the long, warm walk. I sorted the lures into a few in each pocket, and the spinning gloves and the bulk of lures (I always carry plenty anyway) stayed in the small haversack I carried. The spring balance went in one outside pocket of the bag, and my little camera and hand rag into another. Now I was ready: were there pike, or was that a flash in the pan?

The time was about 2.20pm, though I don't remember checking. The next cast went to exactly the same spot. At four-and-a-half seconds I started to retrieve and the Lizard was hit immediately by a fish that leapt almost three feet in the air. Another lively fight and this fish weighed in at 8lb+, this time hooked in the very tip of the lower jaw by one point only of the treble. A couple of casts to the same place produced a lively take and a smaller fish of about 5lb – it was to prove the smallest of a hectic one-and-a-bit days! I had another fish of 6lb+ from the same swim, and then made a move downstream by ten yards or so. As a matter of fact a lot of pike fishermen move too quickly after taking pike from a swim. Whilst it is true that the first one or two casts in a swim are often crucial, they are crucial for the most actively feeding fish in that swim. Quite often there's another bigger fish prepared to feed with a bit of a stimulus – like the sound and fury of a smaller pike being played in. If you move on too quickly one of the results is that you'll cream off the feeding fish on a water, but they do not include the better fish actually prepared to feed.

So I moved very slowly downstream, a few yards at a time, often casting back upstream the way I had come, covering water I had previously fished. I took fish steadily, mostly in the 7–9lb bracket, but also several double-figure fish up to 13lb. The highlight came when I missed a quite savage take just under the rod tip. It was so obviously a big fish, that I sank quietly and slowly to my knees, then crept away to a position five or six yards upstream. I cast back along the bank, beyond the point of the take, and then wobbled the Lizard back nice and slowly. As it passed the point where I had seen the fish, the lure was taken almost casually, and it was well taken. The fight was less spectacular but powerful and I eventually netted a really fine fish of just over 18lb.

What was interesting was that these fish were fighting like summer pike, though they were all a few pounds heavier than they'd be in the summer. I put this down to the increasingly mild conditions after ten days of low temperatures and five days of quite hard frosts. Most of these

One wonders, sometimes, what it is that triggers a feeding response in pike! Photo: David Overy

fish fell to the Lizard, but I'd had some of them on Pikkos and, as I was testing these at the time for Tony Perrin. I continued to swap and change as I walked along. I always change lures frequently anyway, so this was nothing abnormal for me.

But all too soon the light faded and it did begin to chill off, and the pike seemed to stop feeding just before dark. I fished on until dark and then headed back on the long walk. The only other event of the afternoon was that whilst trying to take a short cut across a field I fell full length in a ditch of water and got soaked to the skin. The mild weather suddenly turned cold! As I drove back in the still dense fog I worked out a plan for the following day... I wasn't going

to miss out on a possible continuation of the feeding spell.

My plan was simple: to continue where the pike had stopped feeding, on the assumption that that's what it was, rather than having moved out of a feeding area. My problem was that the walk was a long one, and for a full day I'd need food and drink too. Furthermore the walk would be even longer on the return journey, in the dark. I decided to go in further downstream, to another access that I had through the kindness of a farmer, and then walk upstream to the point where I had run out of takes. Then, working downstream would bring me nearer the car as the day wore on. It meant a very long walk to start with, but at least I'd be fresh and my load would get lighter as I ran out of food and drink! Of course, if the fish were not on the feed, or I'd moved away from the feeding area, then I'd have blown it...

Next day the journey took even longer in the dark. There was no change at all in the conditions, and the barometer was on a peak. I parked as quietly as I could so as not to disturb the farmer, then set off on the lone walk. The going was relatively easy, and it became pleasanter as the light began to filter through. I saw a fox trotting along the bank, and he didn't really seem too bothered about me. It took me an hour to reach my starting point, and it was already lighter than I'd hoped. I sat down on a polythene bag and had a welcome coffee and a couple of sandwiches. Total silence when I stopped munching! My hopes for a sunny day after the fog were ill founded. It stayed thickly foggy all day. I didn't see another soul, only birds and another (?) fox.

David Overy, who died in July 2006, a leading contributor to pike angling. Photo: David Overy

The first five or ten casts produced nothing at all and I was just beginning to doubt my decisions and reasoning when a take under the rod lip whipped it down into the water ... and the whole saga began again. I saw no small pike at all, perhaps the average weight being 8–9lb – for I continued to catch doubles too. It was a repeat of the previous afternoon, and I had six fish from swims on two occasions. But I was also getting some better fish: by lunch I had taken two 18lb-plus fish, a seventeen-pounder and three sixteen-pounders. As on the previous day a lot fell to the Lizard, but in the deeper swims I used the Pikkos to their full effect. You do tend to lose count in these situations, but I do remember counting twenty-four or twenty-six fish the previous day. And on this full day I had a lot more, my counting being about fifty-four fish. The highlight indeed was just before lunch when a fish of 22lb took the Lizard. And later on I had another good fish of 18½lb. Very few fish were lost: one ran for four or five yards then fired the spoon free. I didn't weigh every fish under 10lb, but the afternoon of the first day I took seven doubles, and the second trip produced fifteen doubles. The twenty-four and twenty-six fish would have weighed in excess of 250lb: the fifty-four fish weighed a total of about 550lb, my biggest bag of fish ever in a day: and fifteen is my biggest total of doubles in a day. So we are talking about eighty fish for around 800lb in one-and-a-half days' piking – all on lures. Crazy fishing.

The reason for the feeding spree was the change to mildness. I do think the fog was irrelevant. Using baits I'm sure I'd have had plenty of fish, perhaps more bigger ones too, but I wouldn't have caught so many because the procedures of bait fishing are necessarily slower. Lastly, my most enjoyable take! I'd had one cast into a new swim, and had counted down seven seconds before it hit the bottom. The next cast I started counting, forgot, and after twelve seconds realized it shouldn't still be sinking! In fact, an 18lb fish was swimming along holding the spoon in its jaws – I struck, hooked, and landed it! I didn't have too far to walk back in the dark, but it was an enjoyable walk none-the-less.

The Ultimate Bag

For me, I hasten to add I have chosen the most idyllic of times and places to pen this account of what is to date one of my biggest single bags of pike. It is August 5th 1986, the first summery day of the year and it is dying slowly by the banks of the river. The sun seems to hang on to the last, almost depressing the horizon, the water surface is calm, with a whisper of breeze, and I haven't yet thought about pulling on a sweater to see me through until midnight when I shall stop piking. The farmer is still moving straw past my car parked in his yard. The baits are out, the starlight indicators hang ready to break as the dark comes. Because there has been no action for two hours one can breathe in the atmosphere, and relax. A big pike will introduce some chaos.

What a contrast to March the 8th 1988 when from arriving at the water at 2pm until action slowed at 5pm it was all chaos. Should you ever get that feeling of doubt as to whether it's worth making the trip on the day, when one half of you feels the urge to be up and away, and the other half thinks you ought to attend to some work or domestic tasks, then my advice is to go. Domestic tasks will wait, the ultimate catch will not. Part of my problem had been that my heavy teaching load for the year had only ended the previous week. I still had meetings to attend on the Monday. I had to see my accountant at lunch on Tuesday. Was Tuesday pm, post lunch until dark, really on? Shouldn't I have gone at dawn and come back before lunch? Well I didn't. I'm one of that strange band of people that likes peace of mind before I go fishing. Fishing does not give me peace if I am disturbed beforehand. What's more I do not believe others when they tell me this is what fishing does for them anyway. Though I felt vaguely uneasy, I went fishing. I had a good bag of sardines and smelt and some really good, sparkling herrings and one equally good mackerel. And it was a lure water, and I had my winter lure bag too.

The day itself was unremarkable, perhaps slightly milder than it had been of late, not exactly dull and even with a little sun at times.

I excused myself after lunch and shot away home, changed rapidly and away. I pulled into the parking spot the farmer keeps for me, set off down the side of the ditch, and promptly stumbled and fell in. I remember doing that once with a tub of livebaits. This time I had no excuse. It must have been rather warmer than I thought for I was sweating by the time I reached the water. My ex-SAS rucksack has a weight proportional no doubt to the fitness of its previous owner, and at times I could do with something rather lighter. To save a bit of precious time I upended the rucksack and tipped the lot out on to the grass!

My objective was to have two rods fishing within five minutes of arrival, and a third set up and baited to replace any that came out of the water for a tackle change or to unhook a fish. Both rods were 12ft carbon, one a John Watson rod, one a prototype of my own design. Both rods had 15lb BS Platil line, one with ordinary Platil, the other with thin Platil Universal, and I had a ½oz running Arlesey bomb on each line. No float. My idea was to ledger at quite close range, mostly less than ten yards, and to recast regularly into slightly different places – different by a yard or two. The third rod I never managed to set up, as you shall learn ...

Both rods had size 8 snap tackles on, not barbless, and the upper (or Ryder) hook slid loosely enough on the trace that it made not the slightest kink in the PDQ wire. Although each snap tackle was about 12in long, they were in fact attached to a second trace, also 12in long, so that the total length of wire was 2ft. This had nothing to do with snags at all, but is the method I adopt almost totally nowadays, whether deadbaiting or livebaiting. It simply avoids any risk of bite offs due to the bait flipping back (or up) and hanging over the monofil. The last bite off I had was a day I caught a twenty-seven-pounder with Colin Dyson. Colin also had a twenty that day, and my other run might have been ... that was eighteen months ago. I don't intend having another. Certainly it hasn't adversely affected results as I've had over 400 pike since then.

The first rod ready, I baited up with a sardine, whole (you can get big sardines these days). I set out a buzzer a couple of yards away (on low buzz). A back rod rest wasn't needed with the slope of the bank, so I set the rod on one, clipped up the line and hung the drop back indicator on the line above the butt ring for good measure. Like most of today's pike anglers I like to know exactly what's happening down there – early.

I was just contemplating that I had three hours of good light left (and things often go quite dead anyway in the last hour or so at this time of the year), and was rummaging around for my knife to cut the big herring in two, when the buzzer peeped (one of mine sounds like Road Runner out of breath). I turned around to see the drop back plastic tube creeping slowly up to the second ring, very slowly, and the buzzer light was on but the buzzer itself did not sound, as can happen. On this water it is necessary to strike immediately, so I engaged the pick up still on a little slack line (this automatically removing the line from the clip), removed the drop back coil with one hand, wound down steadily and struck hard. A tremendous boil erupted, seemingly under the rod tip, but actually some ten yards away, and a tail showed momentarily in the air. Then it was away along the bank churning up debris and weed (that I had thought was all dead). The water is perhaps 2ft deep, maybe three in places, so I knew I had a good fish on, and it was several long runs later that I got it near the net. During the playing I had slid tentatively down the bank on my bottom, feet finding anchor in soft mud at the water's edge. A very solid fish slid over the net first go. Now the problem was to climb up the bank. In the end I took the pick-up off the reel and threw the rod, javelin fashion, to the top of the bank. Then, grasping what vegetation would hold the combined weight of me and the fish, which incidentally was still intent on going in the opposite direction, I struggled to the top of the bank, still sweating. I hadn't yet got my breath back since arriving.

The pike was hooked firmly in the scissors, not the easiest place from which to remove hooks though giving you a very reliable hold of course. It weighed in at 14¾lb, and was as fat as any pike I had seen, including trout-water fish! Yet it certainly wasn't bloated with spawn. It was equally tricky returning the fish, which I managed by sliding it down some grass that went all the way to the water.

I threw off the Barbour to get some air! (There are those, who purport to be friends, who say I should throw it off permanently!) This time I chopped a giant sardine in half and swung out the bait about ten yards to the right of the previous cast. Quickly I put the head half of a herring, chosen because it was bright red in places, exactly where the fourteen-and-three-quarter-pounder came from.

I mopped my brow of sweat, using a rag I found in the heap of debris masquerading as tackle ... and the herring-rod buzzer peeped again. I don't know about Road Runner's breath, but mine was none too good at this precise moment. (Incidentally, I do a great deal of long distance running, but I'm never so out of breath as I can get whilst angling!) I slapped on the pick-up as the drop-back tube reached the second rod ring, wound up quickly, but hadn't completed the manoeuvre when the rod whipped hard to the left and the pike took off in a sprint that made Linford Christie look like a baby on all fours. Twenty yards further along the bank there was a boil and things never intended to float again surfaced in an evil looking swirl. I was pondering the boil with some awe, trying to recover slack (for the fish had turned faster than a swimmer at the end of a length), when I saw a massive pike pass me, going the other way to my scramblings down the bank! I caught up with it fairly quickly, only to have a repeat performance. Now, though, it stayed away from me, thumping and shaking the rod. Then I kidded it slowly back to me and, to my enormous relief, it went into the net first time for all the world like a heavy old lady slumping into an armchair.

It had one final flurry as I failed, first time, to lift the fish from the water, and spray went for yards in all directions, adding to my already damp

ABOVE: *Dave Lumb with a 16lb 7oz fish, 1985, and spectacular back drop. Photo: Dave Kelbrick*

LEFT: *Mick Brown, in our view the most complete pike angler ever, with a fish of 34lb on a trolled Rapala Supershad at Blithefield, March 2005. Photo: Mick Brown*

BELOW: *Nigel Grassby with 32-pounder from Pitsford. Photo: Dave Kelbrick*

ABOVE: *Dave Scarf, pioneer jerkbait angler, in 1993 on Lure Angler's Society fish in with a 26½-pounder, Esthwaite Water. Photo: Dave Kelbrick*

TOP LEFT: *Nige Williams with a 31½-pounder, 2003. Photo: Nige Williams*

TOP RIGHT: *Nige Williams with a 38½-pounder. Photo: Nige Williams*

ABOVE: *Nige Williams with a 32½-pounder, 1995. Photo: Nige Williams*

LEFT: *Malcolm Bannister with a 23½lb fish from Esthwaite, as featured in the video,* Success with the Lure, *with Barrie Rickards.*

ABOVE: *Malcolm Bannister enjoying the grandeur of the scenery on Loch Awe near Kilchurn castle. Photo: Malcolm Bannister*

LEFT: *Barrie Rickards with a good lure-caught summer pike from a Fenland drain. Photo: Barrie Rickards*

RIGHT: *Barrie Rickards with a good 20-pounder on deadbait, from a small lake. Photo: Barrie Rickards*

LEFT: *John Watson, one might rightly say the legendary John Watson, author, epitome of the new breed of pike angler, piking guide, and past Secretary of P.A.C. Photo: John Watson*

ABOVE: *The late Tim Cole, and Barrie Rickards, celebrating a 20-pounder in traditional style. Photo: Barrie Rickards*

LEFT: *John Watson with a very big Norfolk pike. Photo: John Watson*

ABOVE: *Barrie Rickards with a fenland 25-pounder on deadbait. Photo: Barrie Rickards*

LEFT: *Dave Steuart in his mid-70s, still catching big ones. Photo: Dave Steuart*

RIGHT: *Derek McDonald with a 29lb fish.* Photo: Angling Times

BELOW: *Eddie Turner with a magnificent brace of 34¼lb and 32¼lb from the Tesco pit.* Photo: Eddie Turner

BOTTOM: *Eddie Turner with a 30½-pounder from Bluebell Lake.* Photo: Eddie Turner

BELOW RIGHT: *Gordon Burton with a big Lakeland pike.* Photo: Gordon Burton

Eric Edwards with a 37½-pounder. Photo: Eric Edwards

Eric Edwards with his splendid 41½-pounder. Photo: Eric Edwards

BELOW: *Denis Moules with a fish of 24lb 15oz from the river Cam. Denis is a Regional Coordinator of P.A.C., a past Regional Organizer, and Fenland piker and extraordinary chronicler. Photo: Denis Moules*

BELOW: *John Milford, past P.A.C. and L.A.S. officer, with 31½-pounder from Bough Beech Reservoir on touch-trolled livebait. Photo: John Milford*

LEFT: *Bill Winship, recent President of P.A.C., with a big 20-pounder from Yorkshire's River Ure, 2004. Photo: Bill Winship*

RIGHT: *Club evening at Ripon P.A.C.*
Photo: Bill Winship

BELOW: *Phil Wakeford (right), Pike Angler of the Year, 2004, being presented with his prize by Bill Winship, then President of P.A.C.*

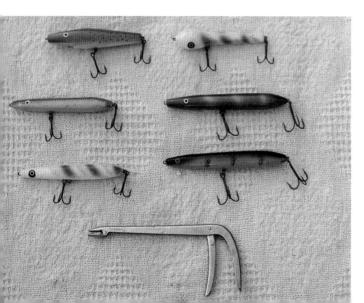

TOP: *Phil Wakeford with a fish of 30lb 6oz from an Irish lough, on lure. He had a fish of 20½lb on the previous cast. Photo: Phil Wakeford*

ABOVE LEFT: *Phil Pearson, with a fish of 32¼lb, 1993. Photo: Phil Pearson*

ABOVE: *Dr John Tate, founder member of P.A.C., past Regional Organizer, with a 20-pounder from the River Wye. Photo: John Tate*

LEFT: *Dave Scarff's Fish Eagle lures, pioneer UK jerkbaits: top left, The Pig; top right, Billy Bomb. Remainder are small and large Top Doctors. Photo: Malcolm Bannister*

discomfort. Then, damn it, the struggle up the banks had to be repeated. I got there on my hands and knees! The fish was beautifully hooked inside the 'cheek', the Ryder having moved to take purchase, the tail treble being free, without a hook hold. In shape it was a repeat of the first fish, in weight it was clearly greater and weighed 24lb.

Now. I don't know about you, but a fourteen-and-three-quarter-pounder is more than enough to make a day's piking for me, so I was now more than happy. I returned the pike very quickly by the same route as the first. I wasn't going to be able to relax in pleasure ... I had made what turned out to be a good decision, namely putting the balance and forceps in my trouser pocket to unhook and weigh at the foot of the bank. Suddenly the half sardine rod 'sounded'! I threw out the half sardine I'd just put on to the other tackle, almost hurled it onto the rod rest, and ran like hell the five yards to the second rod. It's worth

emphasizing that on this water the pike swallow the bait immediately. It's got nothing whatever to do with prebaiting as it's been like that since the very first day I fished it.

That it was another great fish was made quickly obvious and it simply repeated the battling tactics of its predecessors. By now the water for twenty yards to the left and right, and for a similar distance out from the bank, looked like a shell hole of muddied water and drifting debris and weed. I netted that fish equally well, after some very powerful runs, and it weighed 21½lb. A replica, in shape, of its assembled companions. This time the bankside 'over the top' tactics were unnecessary. Not that I wasn't soaked to the skin with sweat by now.

There was then a lull. I set up both rods without interruption ... got my seat out of the heap of rubbish ... took my idiot hat off and mopped my brow with the stinking rag ... retrieved my

David Overy in full battle dress with a big twenty-pounder from Ireland. Photo: David Overy

sandwiches from where I had trodden on them ... started to tidy up the bomb site – then it started again! First one buzzer went, then the other. By now I had it down to a fine art, hitting the fish firmly, sliding down the bank on my arse, rod held high and bent, landing net in left hand or thrown ahead of me. Once, both rods went simultaneously. I struck one, removed the pick-up, and left it ... they both weighed 19lb plus. Then another terrific battle. I saw the fish, knew it was another twenty, so played with it. It didn't with me! That one weighed in at 22½lb; and this became the first time in my life I'd had three twenties in one day, though I've done the pair six times now.

Just before 5.00pm things went dead, or relatively so because I did have another one not long after 6.00pm. I was chilling very quickly because my clothes were soaked. I had had a lit-

tle time to get organized. I jotted the weights down on a card from the rucksack side pocket. Later, I added them up, three twenties, plus nine doubles, for 226½lb, and that included two nineteen-pounders. I've had 200lb bags before, but this was the heaviest (and quickest, in under three hours); and I've shared in bigger catches (including 102 between three of us in two days!); but this was surely, for me, the ultimate bag. Not a run was missed. Each fish was beautifully hooked. And each fish was beautiful ...

As I gathered the debris of the afternoon into a manageable load, and stood to my feet shouldering it, I looked down and saw the other half of that first herring, lying in the grass. All the other fish fell to sardine. I stooped down to pick it up, and the SAS rucksack pulled me off balance and down the slope I went, thankfully for the last time that day ... life goes stumbling on.

David Overy with a summer-caught twenty-pounder from Ireland. Photo: David Overy

And the Gods Roared

I've never been all that taken with ideas about star signs and omens but I have noticed that when fishing arrangements go haywire, with silly and bizarre happenings, the subsequent fishing, if you get any, is sometimes outstanding.

Probably it is just chance. But think back, and I'll bet you can relate some spectacular captures to something that went wrong earlier in the day. Let me give an example. Years ago Ray Webb used to drive from Sheffield to Hull, pick me up, and then we'd fish for the day before he dropped me off and returned home. Those were the days when all I owned was a bike.

On this particular winter morning Ray picked me up well before dawn and we set out for Newport, East Yorkshire, to fish a lake close to what is now the famous Motorway (carp) Lake.

We'd only gone a few miles when the old engine began to snatch and we had to pull into a garage ... and wait for it to open! Three hours later the points had been changed and we were on our way, finally arriving just before lunch, hours after our planned dawn start. We had one of the best half-a-day's piking we'd ever had. So now I try to take trying circumstances more philosophically. Not that it's easy.

So why all this memory stuff? Well, on January 22nd 2000, I had one of those strange days that will live with me forever. First, I overslept by fifteen minutes, which is unusual for me. This was to have real consequence. I arrived at my parking place fifteen minutes later than planned. It was not too late to seriously affect sport because it was still dark and I had plenty of time, or so I thought? The wind was cold, south-westerly and strong and there were big, black clouds about. But, so what, most of our winters are like this now and my walk to the swim would take less than five minutes?

But halfway across the first ploughed field a torrential rainstorm hit me. Within seconds the leaky parts of my one-piece suit were letting in water. Moments later the rain turned to serious hail, and then to heavy snow. The problem now was that I couldn't see a yard in front of me, and

the fields are surrounded by 10ft-deep ditches. I decided that all I could do was camp!

I knelt down on the ploughed soil, got out the brolly and pulled it down as low as it would go. There I sat out the storm, which lasted fifteen minutes. Had I not overslept I would already have been comfortably in my chosen swim, underneath the brolly, instead of being crouched like a fool in the middle of a field.

When the snow stopped I crawled out from under my mushroom and prepared to move, only to realize that one glove was missing, as was my bungie strap that I'd tied up the quiver with, and I was cold and a bit wet. I decided to go on. The decision wasn't based upon the kind of thinking with which I began this article, more out of cussedness. I finally got to the waterside an hour after I'd planned to and it was already showing light in the east. The banks were highly treacherous with the snow and hail (which didn't thaw all day), so I opted for my second choice swim because it was a shorter walk.

So there I was, eventually set up at 7.30am, two deadbaits out in front and attempting to tidy my somewhat damp and disorganized gear. There's only one thing to do at a time like this: cook a breakfast of bacon and eggs. By 8.15 I was well fed, warm, reasonably sheltered and the wrath of the Gods was behind me.

In fact the Gods were beginning to smile. At 8.25 I registered something I least expected under the circumstances – a bite! The float above my popped-up half mackerel was sailing away across the water, and the strike was met with a most solid weight. As so often happens the fish came in fairly easily for a while but when nearer the rod it really began to fight. Also, it felt very heavy; when it stopped running it was difficult to move. The scrap certainly lasted five minutes at close range. Then it came slowly to the surface and I popped it into the net first time. It was a huge fish, clearly a big twenty. It wasn't exceptionally fat, but long and solid. I had great difficulty getting up the bank with it, and when I weighed it I realized why – 31½lb and my fourth Fenland thirty over many years!

Table 2. THE NOTABLE PIKE ANGLERS' BIG PIKE LIST

Name	40+	35+	30+	25+	20+	30/20	VEN	20s per annum	Best fish	Correct to
E.Turner		2	18	41	110	1:6.1	26	4.80	37-08	May-00
M.Brown			19	64	234	1:12.3	51	6.30	35-02	Mar-05
D.Horton		1	14	53	182	1:13	28	7.90	37-04	Apr-05
N.Fickling	1	3	12	93	372	1:31	68	8.95	41-06	Feb-06
D.McDonald		5	17						37-00	Nov-06
N.Williams	2	4	21	47	163	1:7.8	45	5.10	41-04	Mar-05
J.Housden		1	9	26	56	1:6.2	16	1.55	35-00	May-04
P.Pearson		3	10	56	230	1:23	13	8.80	39-12	Jul-04
P.Morgan		1	8	22	107	1:13.4	15	3.82	38-00	May-05
B.Palmer		1	10	52	241	1:24.1	32	6.70	36-08	Apr-05
P.Wakeford		1	7	38	152	1:21.7	38	5.85	37-00	Apr-05
B.Ingrams	1	2	8	24	68	1:4.75	17	2.26	43-02	Apr-05
N.Peat		1	7	51	234	1:33.4	35	8.07	37-01	Apr-05
R.Lyons			7	25	94		12		34-08	Apr-03
M.Carter			7	12	72	1:10.2	9	2.50	32-12	Apr-05
S.Wells			8	39	122	1:16.5	11	3.80	32-04	Sep-04
K.Crow		2	6		96	1:11.8	11		38-00	Mar-01
J.Gardner		2	7	25	114	1:14.4	10		38-08	Mar-01
R.Hughes			6	16	82	1:13.6		3.70	34-04	Apr-00
E.Edwards	1	3	5							May-02
S.Marshall			7	31	100	1:14.2	17	6.25	34-06	Apr-05
M.Ackerly		2	9	27	100	1:11.7	17	5.00	37-04	Apr-05
J.Watson		1	5	57	192	1:38.4	32	5.65	38-01	May-05
A.Rawlings			8	68	278	1:34.75	38	11.12	32-09	Apr-05
B.Rickards			6	34	225	1:37.5	36	4.60	35-08	Apr-05
M.Aggio			8	39	122	1:15.3	13	6.80	34-02	Jul-04
R.Smyth		2	5	25	131	1:26.2	14		36-04	Apr-05
D.Aggio			4	13	75	1:18.75	8	3.00	34-12	Apr-05
B.Culley			3	12	59	1:19.7	15	2.30	33-14	Apr-01
J.Culley			3	8	16	1:5.3	7	1.23	34-02	Apr-01
N.Wheater			3	12	64	1:21.3	11	4.26	31-08	Mar-01

Name	40+	35+	30+	25+	20+	30/20	VEN	20s per annum	Best fish	Correct to
O.Figgis		1	3	9	59	1:19.7	12		36-08	Apr-05
K.Fox		1	5	29	133	1:26.6	19	7.82	35-12	Sep-04
G.Higgins			5	28	138	1:27.6	13	3.60	32-12	Apr-05
P.Sullivan			3	20	91	1:30.3	10	3.90	32-00	Apr-01
D.Overy		1	6	30	134	1:22.3	16	8.38	38-00	Jan-04
K.Shore		3	4	15	66	1:16.5	13	3.00	35-12	May-05
M.Bannister			4	9	38	1:9.5	11		33-04	Apr-05
B.Winship			2	6	64	1:32	14		32-00	Jun-05
J.Matthews		2	2	14	137	1:28	12	4.40	37-00	Jan-01
P.Henry		2	4	24	115	1:29	23	5.00	37-12	May-05
B.Giles			2	20	66	1:33	12	1.32	31-08	Apr-01
P.Haywood			2	22	77	1:38.5	20	2.75	32-09	Mar-01
J.Davis		2	6	35	161	1:26.8	26	8.90	37-00	Apr-04
S.Rodwell			2	25	130	1:65	15	6.50	31-13	Mar-05
A.Shreeve			1	17	95		15	6.30	32-06	Mar-01
R.Sandys			1		44	1:44			30-00	Apr-01
B.Hankins			1	13	85	1:85	20	3.01	30-03	Apr-05
A.Ritchie			1	21	83	1:83	9		30-08	Apr-05
C.Turnbull				23	61		13	1.65	29-10	Jan-01
B.Williams			2	52	143	1:71.5	28	3.48	33-04	Aug-04

A controversial list of the catches of big fish by modern pike anglers compiled by Neville Fickling and regularly updated. The list has a basic voluntary component so quite a few of the anglers mentioned in this book will be missing. Even so, it serves to show just how successful modern pikers are.

Nowadays I carry a throwaway camera on my fishing trips, simply to save weight when walking. I laid the pike on the landing net, on the grass, and was just about to click the shutter when the previously docile biggie leapt smoothly down the grassy banks, as smooth as an otter slide, and ended up with its head in the water and body just on the bank.

I leapt down in pursuit, less than smoothly, camera held up in air. I didn't know whether to take a picture and be done, or take the pike up the bank. Whilst I hesitated the pike didn't, it flipped again, this time landing with its head on the bank and tail in the water. It was covered in mud. I took a picture quickly, and as though the flash was a signal the great pike U-turned and swam off as though it had done this sort of thing all its life. And I had just shot the last frame on the film! It really did look as though things were turning my way. It didn't matter what happened now, of course, because my day, my 'season', had been made, so I sat back to watch the two floats, fill in my diary and have a celebratory cuppa. All went quiet ... At 11.10 I had a good run on a giant half-mackerel head, but after bending into the fish it bumped off. It felt a heavy fish. Nowadays, one of my tricks is not to re-cast the bait straight after a bump-off, but to put a lure through the swim. Today my lure rod (made up ready like the rest of my tackle) had on it a Rapala Shad Rap from the previous week. I chucked it in the vicinity of the hotspot and on only the second cast it was taken with a mighty thump. A spectacular fight ensued with a lot of diving and spiralling, and it was only late in the fight that I realized it was another very heavy fish, when it sulked and I could hardly move it at all. Then the fish surfaced, remained quiet, and for the second time that day a big fish popped easily into my 32in-diameter round net! This time I weighed it by the waterside: 31½lb. Surely the same fish! I had measured the first one at 44in long, and this one measured 45in. Nor could I see the split in the tail that I had seen as the first biggie neared the net. Even so ...?

The fish swam calmly away and clearly wasn't the slightest bit bothered at being captured. I found that, this time, I couldn't fish on. I'd had an amazing day, and now was the time to pack up slowly and carefully and head off home. As I sat in the car and switched on the engine the now gale force winds became reinforced with heavy rain. Packing up was a good decision.

7 A NEW BREED OF PIKE ANGLER

Earlier in the book we outlined how the whole pike-angling scene was fundamentally transformed in the late 1950s and early 1960s from the primitive bait and lure fishing of the past to the sport we have today, the revolution in modern lure fishing perhaps lagging a decade behind that in bait fishing. We have mentioned the anglers and the contributions they made at the very beginning of the revolution – Bill Giles, Fred Taylor and so on. The ideas propagated by these people were rapidly taken up by other anglers who recognized the positive changes taking place and recognized the discoveries. They also recognized the catches, as we briefly outlined in the previous chapter. Results inspire people!

When you look at a list of these people it now reads like a *Who's Who?* of pike angling. We apologize if we have missed anyone out, but we can only record as we feel, based upon those anglers who have recorded their approach through articles and books, given lectures to societies, simply reported their catches to the press, or who are otherwise well-known to us. One or two we have deliberately missed out in this chapter because they appear elsewhere in a different context.

Neville Fickling

Let's begin with the most famous of them all, and at times the most controversial, namely Neville Fickling. He followed close on the heels of Barrie and Ray Webb in the early 1960s, almost literally at times! He has become the most successful pike angler in history, bar none. With more big pike than anyone else by a big margin, he has long overtaken Dennis Pye's 1960s record (Dennis was the most successful

piker ever until Neville came along). Neville is rather modest about his achievements in piking, claiming that he hasn't done much except catch fish, hasn't discovered anything if you like. We correct this elsewhere in the book but even if it were wholly true it ignores the fact that he has led by inspiration. Many pike anglers, including some in this chapter, are out there now, succeeding because Neville, more than anyone, showed them that it could be done, with drive, initiative and application. This last point is a thread we shall return to in the last chapter but for the moment we shall leave it with Neville. Lastly we should mention his books, *Pike Fishing* (1992), *In Pursuit of Predatory Fish* (1986), *Pike Fishing in the 80s* (1982) and so on, and many articles in the press on all matters of piking. In our opinion it all adds up to a very major contribution to piking.

Mick Brown

Mick Brown is considered by many, including ourselves, to be perhaps the greatest pike angler ever. He recently passed Barrie's total of twenty-pound pike captures and is snapping at Neville's heels, but more than that has contributed very considerably to pike-angling development, whether in bait or lure fishing. His book, *Pike Fishing: the practice and the passion* (1993), is an excellent testament to his contribution. And more so than many leading anglers, he tends not to follow the 'going' water but fishes his own way. As several others on our list of the new breed of pike anglers, he is a professional angler and, like John Watson, sets high professional standards.

John Watson

John Watson, blunt and occasionally controversial, has always brought a high level of commonsense and practicality to his fishing, and his classic tome, *A Piker's Progress* (1991), is as good and as valuable a read now as when it was first published. Another good one was *Pike* (1989), in the Master Fisherman series. John also did a very successful stint as Pike Anglers' Club Secretary, and through his guiding business has proved extremely helpful and instructive to many inexperienced pike anglers – we know this because they have informed us.

John Watson is not only a renowned guide but has now taken 192 twenty-pounders and five thirty-pounders since he started piking in earnest in 1973, although he actually began piking in the late 1960s on the Lancaster Canal. Later he fished the Lincolnshire drains, partly because colleagues in the National Anguilla Club, who fished there, were happy to help him. He met Bob Jackson (who made Barrie a superb set of rod rests, still in use) and Mick Brown and they fished together often over the next four years, from 1973. You can well imagine how productive a period this was, not just for them, but also for piking. And when, not long after, John teamed up with Malcolm and with Gordon and Barrie Burton, the road to success was mapped out by higher powers. John joined P.A.C. in 1977, moved to Norfolk in 1980 and has been there ever since. In 1980 he was P.A.C. 'Pike Angler of the Year'. John was responsible for P.A.C. immediately after Barrie, Hugh Reynolds and Bill Chillingsworth, and along with Martyn Page and Vic Bellars took the

Packy Joe Reynolds, famous Irish pike angler, oversees posing with a 25¾lb fish. Photo: George Higgins

*George Higgins with a 18½lb fish on a silver montblanc,
11 September 1990. Note how slim they both are.
Photo: George Higgins.*

*Derrick Amies with his fantastic 42lb 2oz fish
from the River Thurne, Norfolk, August 1985.
Photo: Derrick Amies*

club to new heights. This was when the magazine, *Pikelines*, was formed: previously it had been the Pike Anglers' Club magazine. John's contribution to P.A.C. was immense, of that there is no doubt; and in the 1980s he had great success as a pike angler, but always putting something back into the sport, not least being his book, *A Piker's Progress* and, later, his guiding. This last he started simply as a job, but soon realized that it was both a marvellous medium for teaching beginners at piking, and one which gave him a lot of pleasure. Today, he is a more laid-back pike angler than up to the late 1980s! He's continued a lot of good work through his column in the *Norwich Eastern Evening News*, where the welfare of pike is often mentioned. Today, John fishes quietly, mostly on his own, and has an aversion to anglers who move on to a 'going' water, live on it until it's finished, and then move.

John Sidley

The late John Sidley, specialist in river fishing and the River Severn in particular, brought an astonishing enthusiasm to his piking as well as an ability to catch large numbers of big fish. In his too brief stay on the scene he was possibly the most likeable and unaffected character in the game. His book, *River Piking* (1987), remains a classic. Barrie was responsible for editing the book and attempted to do this whilst preserving the essential John Sidley, and struggling at the same time with the fact that John was relatively uneducated and the text really needed work on it. Malcolm tried very hard to get John to do a talk at a P.A.C. conference. He would always refuse, he said his nerves would get the better of him. Malcolm, like John Sidley, left school at fourteen without any qualifications, and Malcolm also found public speaking quite an ordeal. He did, however, have a strong interest in history and left school top of the class with a pass mark of 87 per cent – hence his interest in pike-fishing history.

Eddie Turner and Jim Housden

Eddie Turner we have spoken of elsewhere. Suffice it to say here that his open and questioning approach, asking fundamental questions to boot, is rather unusual and is probably the main factor behind his innovative approach to piking and his discoveries. He also has a knack of catching big fish, and wrote a super book, *Mega Pike* (1990). Jim Housden we group with Eddie only in the sense that at one stage they caught very big fish from the same Essex lake. Jim is one of the quieter ones, rarely writing, but hunting out big pike in a range of waters both in England and Ireland. He loves the big waters and has done well on them. Barrie has fished a fair bit with Jim and

Martyn Page and John Wilson with good fish. Photo: Martyn Page

recognizes an angler who gets his tackle and techniques as near perfect as possible. There is a tendency towards this in all the anglers in this chapter except, perhaps, Bill Winship.

Bill Winship

Bill Winship is, as we pen this, President of the P.A.C. and like so many in this book has 'done his time' in angling administration to do with pike. Bill is a very successful angler living in the north, and it would not be unfair to describe his tackle as being a bit scruffy. It's good where it matters, of course, especially when it comes to hooks and lures and bait. in addition he brings to pike fishing a rare intuition both as to waters and to the whereabouts of pike in them. His book, *Pike Waters* (1996), was a bit of a first in that it told anglers, broadly speaking, where good piking was to be found. And his writing on pike matters, usually with a slant or perspective not considered by others, is only lacking in that we could do with more of it.

In the north west, pike fishing was quite difficult, some anglers actually migrating to Norfolk, and the Lake District not yet tapped, but some did succeed.

Ron Pendleton

Ron Pendleton was one of the real stalwarts of pike many years ago, although he keeps a low profile these days after being rather badly maligned by a few people during one of those rather too frequent disputes. Ron is a tremendous pike angler, with outstanding results, and yet was able to put in a lot of time to help P.A.C. when it needed it. He was the very first winner of the P.A.C. 'Angler of the Year' in 1979. One of his best catches included five twenty-pounders in a week, and he's also had three twenties in a day; best fish 28lb. In the north west it may have been tricky but in some parts of the Fens things were moving rapidly. For example, Trevor Simpson by 1994 had had 142 twenties and five thirties, all

from Fenland drains in Lincolnshire (as well as a Bough Beech 40½-pounder).

Bill Chillingsworth

Bill Chillingsworth, the very first President of P.A.C. (selected by Barrie and by Hugh Reynolds, then Treasurer) is another very intuitive pike angler. In all Barrie's years of fishing only two pikers have consistently out-fished him on a day's outing and they are Martin Gay and Bill, both amongst the best of those with a deep understanding of where pike might be in a swim. Bill has been a very successful angler, fishing primarily in the Fens and in Cambridgeshire, be it drain, river or gravel pit. His book, *Tactics for Big Pike* (1985), is a small tome of concentrated commonsense and practicality. Of the anglers we know, he first brought the attention of anglers to

Bill Chillingsworth weighing a fish in excess of 21lb, Great Ouse Relief Channel 1960s, when fish were weighed in a different manner. Photo: Barrie Rickards

*Barrie Rickards with a big Loch Lomond fish, 1970s.
Photo: Barrie Rickards*

*Colin Dyson with a twenty-four-pounder from
Nottinghamshire. Photo: Colin Dyson*

the fact that consistent success with livebait was no good unless you had a supply of good baits all the time – preferably very small chub. He was less intuitively successful with deadbaits but *was* good with lures when he chose to employ them. It is fair to say that when the Cambridgeshire Pike Anglers was in existence he was a major, if not *the* major contributor to it, and extremely generous to members in disclosing information about waters and swims. He would *never* fish a swim he knew was someone else's favourite if there was any chance at all they'd be on the water that day. He was deeply upset when it seemed that one of the Cambridge Pike Anglers

was withholding information about a hotspot and we reckon this is the reason the Cambridge Pike Anglers met its end, as indeed did many specimen groups at that time, and for more or less the same reason.

Andy Mundy

The late Andy Mundy, more famous perhaps for big-bream exploits, was also very successful on the Gloucestershire and Wiltshire gravel pike where he took sixty-two twenty-pounders and five thirty-pounders over a ten-year period. Like

Barrie Rickards returning a thirty-pounder.
Photo: Barrie Rickards

so many keen pikers, Andy was a meticulous diarist so we may yet read of more details of a career so sadly cut short.

Derrick Amies

Derrick Amies, who followed in Dennis Pye's Broadland footsteps after a gap of a few years, was, like Bill Chillingsworth, a livebait enthusiast. He brought Pye's dumbbell technique back to piking and became – and still is – a very successful piker and, like Neville Fickling, has caught pike over 40lb from the Broads, joining a rather rare group of the new breed! We have also seen Derrick lure fishing, and can confirm that he knows his onions in that business too. He hasn't produced a book as yet and does not often write articles, although he does give lectures and attends meetings where he seems only too willing to help other anglers. In a recent interview however, he surprised us rather by asking why *should* he write a book and pass on all his secrets. It may have been said tongue-in-cheek, of course,

because most of this new breed of pikers we discuss in this chapter have been seriously generous in passing on their knowledge.

Dave Lumb and Others

Dave Lumb has helped take lure fishing to a new level but is a highly successful bait angler too, producing *Modern Pike Rigs* (1992), as well as numerous helpful articles in magazines such as *Pike and Predators*. Malcolm used to joke that Dave changed his pike rigs more than he changed his underpants. Like Dave we have already dealt with the roles of Gordon Burton, Dave Kelbrick and Charlie Bettell in Chapter 4 on lure fishing, but they could all be included in the concept of the new breed, as could the legendary Derek Gibson, an old friend of ours who also owes the piking world a book or two. Two more lure-fishing contributors who owe us all some writing are Chris Leibbrandt and John Milford, ex-committee men from the P.A.C., both of whom have made enormous contributions to piking since the 1980s, not least with their slide shows and one-day lure-fishing competitions.

Dave Batten and Martyn Page

Dave Batten published *An Introduction to Pike Fishing* in 1989, which is of value to many other than the beginner at piking; and he is rightly lauded for his magnificent illustrations in books and articles. One of the very successful Broads anglers, Dave has also done long spells working for the P.A.C. and for anglers in general. Not only a successful pike angler, he is one of the stalwarts of the sport. Another successful Broadland angler and friend of Dave Batten is Martyn Page, now also a well-known and respected tackle manufacturer. He has also put pen to paper in a most impressive manner with Vic Bellars in *Pike: the Pursuit of Esox lucius* (1989), and with John Bailey in *Pike: the Predator Becomes the Prey* (1985). Martyn also did his stint as a P.A.C. officer along with John Watson and Vic Bellars. It is noteworthy

An active pike on Lough Beg in Northern Ireland.
Photo: George Higgins

a compendium of historical and recent data about what Eddie Turner would call 'megapike'.

Phil Pearson

Phil Pearson is now fifty-five so fits well into our new breed of pike angler, with well over 230 20lb pike to his net, including ten thirty-pounders up to 39lb 12oz. In one season he took 147 double-figure fish and has had ten doubles in a day on two occasions, three twenty-pounders in one day twice, and two twenties in a day on no less than fifteen occasions. And, we know that Phil has caught well over 1,000 pike over 10lb. One of our reasons for giving you some idea as to just how successful our modern pikers are, is to contrast the present with the past: piking is much better nowadays, and one of the reasons has to be that anglers are conserving pike fishing. Phil's 1,000-plus doubles were probably caught as jack pike but have been returned to grow on. Some of them may have become twenty-pounders caught by him, or by others. It's not all about good techniques these days. The fish are there to catch too. He puts a lot of his early success down to reading *Fishing for Big Pike*, and Martin Gay's classic, *A Beginner's Guide to Pike Fishing* (which it isn't of course). Although very successful with baits, Phil has in recent times turned to lure fishing, and has become an expert in making his own plugs; at the same time he has become one of the modern breed of boat anglers.

that many of those great anglers, who often become professionals, have also put back a great deal into the sport by helping to run the major piking club, and other clubs too. Those who criticize today's professional pikers would do well to ponder on this. Martin has landed more than a hundred twenty-pounders, and not far short of that from the Broads: this is a remarkable achievement because few anglers top fifty such fish from the Broads.

Steve Harper

Yet another major player in Broads piking was Steve Harper. His book, *Broadland Pike* (1998), will become a classic before many years are past, not only for the quality of the volume itself, but because of the huge amount of research that Steve did to establish details of the capture of all the giant pike of the region. Add this to the tomes by Fred Buller and Neville Fickling referred to earlier in the book and you have quite

Jim Gibbinson

What is interesting is that many of the books just mentioned, written by the new generation, were published in the 1990s: it really is a new group of highly experienced and contributing anglers following the earlier wave which tended to have books published in the 1970s and 1980s. Some we have dealt with in context at an earlier stage but two we have not mentioned so far. One is Jim Gibbinson's *Pike* (1974), in the Osprey series, which, though concise, was a clear exposition of where we were in the mid-1970s. Jim made a considerable input to piking in those days, providing an invaluable link between some of the pioneers and the new breed of this chapter. Quite probably Jim was the clearest and most logical of thinkers at the time and may not have been bettered. He also stopped serious pike fishing after a while to devote his time to other species, so we have not heard a great deal of him in recent times. Indeed, we remember his polite and friendly resignation from P.A.C. as he moved on to new pastures. He is one of angling's gentlemen.

Ken Whitehead

The second angler referred to above is Ken Whitehead, whose book, *Pike Fishing* (1987), was more or less a piking autobiography. Although Ken (=Deryck Swift) would never have claimed to be a pioneer of the new piking, he began piking around 1950 and fished regularly until his

death in the 1990s. The book is as idiosyncratic as Ken himself was, and you will find in it many offbeat ideas and atypical opinions, exactly the sort of thing we should be exposed to more often. It's worth noting too, that Barrie read an earlier draft of the book than the one finally published, and large sections of seriously good stuff had been taken out by an unappreciative publisher. A great pity.

Barrie fished extensively with Ken and published several books with him. Some have already been dealt with in the lure-fishing chapter, but one gave them a lot of fun and pleasure and that was the photographic guide to basic pike angling, *Pike Fishing Step by Step* (1976). To produce this book Ken and Barrie targeted various waters in Fenland and the Lee Valley, using a whole variety of techniques, but based on their actual fishing, with actual gear: no borrowed, new equipment here! For one shoot Barrie was demonstrating casting, on a Fenland drain. Ken got the picture with the last frame on the film, whereupon Barrie fell in the

Colin Goodge, P.A.C. founder member, Regional Organizer and Chairman, with a 23lb 6oz fish from the River Lark. Photo: Colin Goodge

LEFT: *Neville Fickling, probably the most successful piker ever. Photo: Neville Fickling*

BELOW: *Neville Fickling with a big Ladybower fish. Photo: Neville Fickling*

The late Packy Joe Reynolds, past President of 'The Pikers', on Lough Key during the Irish Pike Championships, won by George Higgins (on the right!). Photo: George Higgins

The top end of Loch Lomond at Ardlui, Barrie's boat and brolly both visible. This bay was a Mecca for many modern pikers thanks to early work by Fred Buller. Photo: Barrie Rickards

drain! Ken struggled to get another film into the camera and asked Barrie to repeat the procedure! He didn't! But what he did do was to change quickly into dry clothes, which in winter he always carries in the back of the vehicle.

John Wilson and Des Taylor – Media Stars

We have not yet mentioned the media stars such as John Wilson and Des Taylor. Their approach to piking is exemplary, both practical and thinking, and they have both managed to translate their knowledge into their respective media elements: John Wilson primarily on TV, but with good books and videos too; Des Taylor mostly with his *Angling Times* column and his videos. The pair are superb adverts for the sport of piking, and put over the very best, not just of piking indeed, but also of angling itself. John always has a conservationist message and is firm yet diplomatic; Des is perhaps tougher, harder on the charlatans in angling but always helpfulness itself to the inexperienced and to beginners. Des won the lure-fishing championship at Thorpe Park with a spectacular catch from beneath the resident paddle boat, an event which went the publicity rounds, rightly so, and the piking grapevine too. Both these men have done piking proud outside the immediate sphere of piking and are typical of, and leaders in, the breed of modern pikers who sell the subject on. P.A.C. as a club, does the same, of course, but individuals have a huge part to play now that pike angling has moved out of its rather inward-looking prehistory. Fred Buller, naturally, is also part of the move to show piking outside the narrower confines of the sport and he is as much part of the modern piker scene as he is a link with the old piking scene.

The idea of using the moon phases to assisting and interpreting pike fishing began relatively recently and we shall leave a fuller discussion of it until the Epilogue near the end of the book. Our attention was first drawn to the possibility by Paul Howells back in the 1980s: he had been keeping records for some time and beginning to form some conclusions.

Mark Barrett, one of the most successful Fenland pikers, with a fish of 23lb from the Sixteen Foot River.

You will have noticed that quite a few piking 'names' have not been mentioned in this chapter, or perhaps mentioned rather briefly. This is because we see a new phase, developing from the 1990s new breed, and this we deal with in Chapter 11 as the new millennium. There you will recognize more faces, such as Nige Williams (*Just Williams*, 2005), among several others, and we shall discuss the manner in which parts of the sport seem to be changing.

8 BIG WATERS

Whether bank or boat fishing, big waters are a challenge. To some extent bank fishing is an extension of what we outlined in Chapters 2 and 3: the angler breaks down the water into manageable sections, perhaps learns some new techniques of distance fishing (Chapter 10) and tries hard to find the reachable hotspots or, if the angler doesn't believe in these, the 'going swims'. It is boat fishing that requires the new mental attitude. Boat fishing we touched upon in Chapter 4 where we discussed its relevance to lure fishing, but boat fishing is the best way to tackle distance, the best way to search a whole water, often the best way to have a peaceful day, and it opens up a series of new vistas for the bait angler.

Boat Fishing

Boat fishing as carried out by the new pikers in the UK is as far from boat fishing in the first half of the last century as you can get. Gone are the leaky, clinker-built, heavy boats: only stability was in their favour. Now we have cabined boats – excellent for shelter or cooking – fibreglass boats, and equipment on them that would make an old timer blanch. Furthermore, increasingly boats are custom-designed for anglers, with wells for bait and angler-friendly seats. The reasons for all this change are that more big waters have become available to pikers, and great successes have resulted.

As always in this book we do want to make a contrast with the past. Up to and including the 1960s boat angling was primitive. True, experienced pikers in Ireland were successful in trolling; and on the Norfolk Broads anglers mostly used boats to reach inaccessible waters. In Northern

Geoff Parkinson with a Lake District whopper.
Photo: Dave Kelbrick

Ireland the Northern Ireland Pike Society (N.I.P.S.) and The Pikers took boat fishing for pike to a new and very successful level. Whilst most of us in England think of George Higgins as the guru, it is important to realize that he was often the spokesman for one of the most successful boat-fishing teams ever. In the 1960s they were still using old-fashioned boats, but they brought the art of trolling to a new pitch entirely.

LEFT: *James Holgate with a good river pike. Photo: Dave Kelbrick*

BELOW: *Gordon Burton wearing his serious face. Photo: Gordon Burton*

Some anglers tried to emulate them in Scotland on Loch Lomond, but most of these anglers ended up bank fishing more often than not.

Of course, as so often is the case, some angling writers were ahead of the game, and if you look in Fred Buller's and Hugh Falkus' book, *Freshwater Fishing* (1975), you will see various boat handling tactics well laid out and illustrated, and these techniques, especially as regards safety, are as valid today as ever they were. Modern boaters may need to adapt some of them slightly to suit the new boats.

Sizing Up a Big Water

Even the boat angler has to break down the size of a big water into smaller sections: he has to know exactly where he is fishing, whether it is a deep trough down the middle of an arm of the lake, or a particular drop-off or promontory. In the old days we would buy Admiralty charts that

were, and probably still are excellent. However, using a modern echo sounder you can prepare your own up to date, accurate, and angler friendly map. Colin Dyson and Barrie did this in the early days on Ardingly Reservoir in Sussex, first of all getting a good outline of the lake from our Ordnance Survey map, and then doing a series of traverses, recording as they went. At all times they knew exactly which feature they were fishing, and why – there was nothing hit or miss about it at all.

Navigation Aids

A GPS (Global Positioning System) also helps. Not that an angler is likely to get lost on even the biggest of UK waters, but when a good taking spot is located it is helpful to know *exactly* where it is. Hotspots of any kind can be very small areas. Prior to the GPS the angler would throw overboard a big float anchored by a strong line

Gordon Burton playing a Loch Lomond pike taken on whole mackerel deadbait. You can almost hear him whoop. Photo: Gordon Burton

and heavy weight. Whilst this is fine on the day it doesn't help much on a repeat visit. A GPS does; because you can plot a route on the GPS and follow it exactly to the site. Again it is fishing to a plan rather than at random. In the past a lot of boat fishing for pike was rather random, although the accumulation of information went on until a picture emerged.

Modern echo sounders can distinguish shoals of small (prey) fish, individual large pike, depths, weed beds and so on. It is certainly very useful to plot areas frequented by large pike even if they are not feeding on the day – and often they are not. We think it was Colin Dyson who first observed, in this country at least, that a big pike in feeding mode was likely to be angled upwards, looking upwards if you like, whereas a horizontally disposed pike was probably not feeding. Echo sounders tell us convincingly that pike in big waters do not spend all their time sitting in deep water on the bottom. They are often at particular depths and in specific places, with or without a recognizable 'feature'. Whilst the echo sounder may tell you the nature of the bottom you can always check this by dropping the anchor.

Outboard Motors

Another aid to modern piking is the electric outboard, a quiet and efficient tool usually brought into play when the preferred fishing area has been located. It certainly gets around Bill Giles' oft-stated worry that, in shallow waters at least, an ordinary outboard can spook the fish in a swim. Outboards themselves have improved considerably and are much more flexible at low speeds, especially four-stroke engines, and you still have the choice of trolling on the oars, at which we are relatively good, having spent years doing it.

Techniques for the Big-Water Angler

There are several main techniques open to the big-water angler. Obviously one is trolling, but not only of artificial, but of dead- and livebaits. The latter is a relatively modern development, at least in detail. Whilst dead fish have always been trolled they were fished in a manner similar to trolled artificials. Nowadays, a trolled bait is likely to be

under a trolling float and set at a specific depth quite carefully. The actual technique is quite skilful and to get the best action out of the trolled bait the speed of the boat is crucial, with due regard to the wind conditions at the time. This is sometimes easier on the oars than it is on the outboards.

Oars

It may be helpful to have a short digression on the subject of oars and of safety. Occasionally you find a boat with the oars fixed in position: when not in use they are laid along the gunwales, where commonly the boat has rowlocks or thole pins, the latter especially in Ireland. Rowlocks should not be left in position when anchored in a powerful current flow, but should be tied securely to the boat so that, even when not in use, they can be hung safely inboard. You can't do this with thole pins, which are bars sticking up from and through the gunwales. They are a potential danger if anchored in flow, but on the other hand you rarely lose an oar when using thole pines. Loss of an oar overboard is dangerous, and is always more likely to happen in rough conditions or conditions when the pike are feeding – a variation on chaos theory!

Lifejackets

Lifejackets or flotation suits do seem a sensible precaution when piking afloat, especially as a majority of fishermen can barely swim. Wearing these is a bit of a nuisance, especially on a hot day, but not a nuisance at all if you are the man overboard. All the serious modern writers advocate them and most films feature them. They'd be useful for Barrie because the distance he can swim is directly proportional to the depth of the water.

Anchoring

Returning now to bait fishing from an anchored boat. Most non-nautical types, ourselves included, find anchoring rather difficult. It's easy enough to hold bottom, by having out enough good anchor rope, a decent anchor, and perhaps a length of chain between anchor and rope. But anglers want the boat to say still, which it rarely does. If there is a known and steady flow direction

ABOVE: *Gordon Burton in less serious mood. Photo: Gordon Burton*

RIGHT: *James Holgate with a nice fish caught boat fishing. Photo: Dave Kelbrick*

Tim Cole preparing the boat for him and Barrie on a Fenland piking session. Photo: Barrie Rickards

Barrie in philosophical mode, on Loch Lomond with lure. Photo: Barrie Rickards

then it is possible to fix the anchor rope amidships. The boat will still swing around, of course, or you can put an anchor from the stern and the bows, much as they used to do with punts when Thames barbel fishing. What you cannot do, except in shallow water and calm conditions, is put the anchors down on a vertical rope. And in shallow water a pole might be as good as a mud anchor. The deeper the water and the stronger the wind or water flow the more rope is needed and the greater the swing on the boat. It is possible, on occasions, to put out a long bow line and a long stern line and have a shorter anchor amidships – but there is still some movement and it takes an age to get in position. All in all, the simplest and most reliable system is to have a longish bow rope out, into the wind, and a shorter stern anchor to steady the swing of the stern a little.

Techniques for Big-Water Anglers

So what do you do? After all it is imperative to keep in close contact with the baits. On the Norfolk Broads quite a number of anglers use multiplier reels, tighten to the bait, and then allow the swing to take place with the reel ticking off line. Any further ticking is then a run! It probably

works well enough on a shallow broad when the swing of the boat is less, but in deeper water it may not work at all. The real answer is to use floats. Although these will drag from time to time if the bait is on the bottom you can at least keep an eye on the float and watch positive action when a pike takes. It doesn't work entirely well in rough weather, but it is better than ledgering. Bait runners help too.

Very few anglers have addressed these problems in their writings, but one who has is the legendary John Wilson, in his excellent little book, *Catch Pike* (1991). In the same book he deals with water coverage when using baits from a static boat. In all these views our ideas are in exact accord with his.

Casting lures from a 'static' boat is, of course, less of a problem in that the tackle is under control in terms of takes, even if you do not have the lure exactly where you'd like it all the time. Given the passage of time, radial casting will cover all the water available to that anchor position even if there's a lot of swing on the anchor rope. All these problems are to do with big waters and really hardly apply to lakes of a few acres. But waters like Corrib, Mask, Allen, Lomond, trout reservoirs,

Gordon Burton with a superb Loch Lomond pike. Photo: Gordon Burton

Boat fishing changed in the 1980s. Even on this small craft, on Ardingly reservoir, Barrie has it well organized.
Photo: Barrie Rickards

the bigger Norfolk Broads, Hornsea Mere, Windermere and others like them do need thought before going afloat.

Some anglers have made their names in part on big waters, such as Gordon Burton who employs advanced lure-fishing techniques and modern boating methods and informed us recently that he had had more than 150 twenty-pounders from such waters. Gordon and Malcolm have fished with another Southport piker, Bob Forshaw, who only boat fishes the big waters. He fishes quietly, but would be well up Neville's 'Big Pike' list. He seems happy enough to go afloat in seriously bad weather, but equips himself for it with a lifejacket. There is a problem with lure fishing in really rough conditions that is nothing to do with safety of the boat. In good hands, a good-sized craft is probably safe enough from capsizing in almost all conditions. No, it's more to do with comfort. You have to ask yourself whether it is enjoyable

for you to land fish, unhook them and return them in conditions where water is slopping over the gunwales. Tim Cole and Barrie nearly won a big pike contest in Ireland by drifting broadside to the waves and allowing the push of the wind and water to work the lures. They caught fish regularly, but playing, 'landing' and unhooking them was neither easy nor enjoyable. It was bruising to the body. There was the ever-present danger of a treble hook penetrating something that wouldn't welcome it, and a consequence was that they did not feel the fish were as well looked after as they might have been. And too much water came over the sides! In short, we both think one cannot fish properly in very rough weather.

Before what we might call the 'Burton' era of boat fishing, we had another rather wild pair in Fred Wagstaffe and Bob Reynolds. Ray Webb fished in Ireland quite a lot with them and considered them to court danger too closely for

Alan Ritchie playing a fish of 23½lb, taken on trolled roach. Photo: George Higgins

his liking. And this was in the days before boats were angler-designed, and generally better equipped and safer. Other anglers pushing boating for pike were Fred Buller (with a lot of Irish experience), Dick Walker and the Taylors and Bill Giles, all on Loch Lomond after its giant pike. Generally, they were using traditional systems, static with baits, although Fred Buller had trolled and spun extensively in Ireland, with good results. Gordon Burton was, indeed is, more innovative with lures and tackle. For example, he, like us, tried using wire lines – these get the lure down quickly and more exactly than monofil, but are not as pleasant to use, at least for us. They seem out of vogue at the moment, possibly because of the rise of braids that can accomplish at least some of the attributes of wire lines.

At this point we would like to mention the work of James Holgate on big-water piking. Many of the aspects we have mentioned above have been considered in some detail by James, who is a vastly experienced big-water angler, possibly the most experienced. He published two small but valuable books: *Big Water Pike Fishing: books 1 & 2* (1989, 1990). We'd strongly recommend these books as amongst the best if you are beginning to fish big waters or getting involved at all in boat fishing. And you could do much worse than purchase two other fine volumes that he did on lure fishing, especially if you plan to combine boats and lures. James Holgate is the epitome of the way big-water piking has improved in recent decades. Two other major contributors, via articles and talks, to the scene of big-water fishing are Eric Edwards, pike catcher extraordinary, and Geoff Parkinson, the latter having done a series in *Pike and Predators* in 2005.

Downriggers

Some techniques, though excellent on their day, never seem to take off fully. Downriggers control precisely the depth at which the lure swims, but in a sense are less flexible for waters where the bottom rises and falls a deal. Without a downrigger one can vary the pace of the boat and raise and lower the rods. But for a long, really deep

This pike prefers the other bank to the boat. Photo: George Higgins

troll over an even lake bottom, downriggers take some beating. Ray Webb used them on the Irish loughs in the 1970s, although it must be said that his downrigger weight constituted a large rock!

Gordon Burton is one of piking's enthusiasts as anyone who has listened to his talks will know. He has been piking now for forty-five years, claiming to have been mesmerized by Fred Wagstaffe whom we have mentioned earlier. He became a specialist piker in the early 1970s and prefers trolling to other lure-fishing methods, having caught them down to 38ft on Loch Woodall. (Barrie once took one in Ireland at 70ft, bouncing a Colorado along the bottom.) Gordon was instrumental in part, in getting anglers up to Loch Lomond and has fished there at almost every time of the year: by 1994 he'd taken twenty-seven fish from Lomond in excess of 20lb of his total of fifty-six twenties at that stage. In fact, in the mid-1990s especially, he had some terrific bags of pike trolling Lomond, both large catches and big fish. His experience at trolling big waters in a range of conditions may be second to none

bar, perhaps, the Northern Irish Pike Society (N.I.P.S.) team. On many occasions Gordon has stated that although he likes all pike fishing he doesn't really feel at home unless he's on big water. Malcolm too, fished Lomond with some success, taking pike to over 26lb. The Fred Buller and Jim Gibbinson books inspired him, both showing large bags of Lomond pike. And who can forget Dave Plummer with that large pike in that evocative photograph taken outside the Tin Boat House at Balmaha? Sadly Lomond has, during the last few years, failed to live up to its former glory. There is a debate as to why the large pike have disappeared. Whatever the reason we hope it comes back as a truly great pike water.

Both Ray and Barrie fished like this on Lough Ree, with only ordinary success, whereas Dave Cumpstone fishing more traditionally and fishing the shallows too, did rather better with fish to 27lb. With downriggers the length of line and trace immediately above the lure is clipped to the downrigger lead, and the rod tip is tightened down so that it bends sharply to the lead. The

Tim Cole and Colin Brett, both past P.A.C. Regional Organizers, about to launch Colin's craft in Fenland.
Photo: Barrie Rickards

George Higgins with his son Michael, and a 24½-pounder taken on 22 April 1989 on a pikelet plug in 2½ft of water.

rod is in a rod holder. Takes are indicated by the rod tip springing straight, something that takes a little getting used to!

Side Planers

Side planers – which we have used on big drains successfully – never seemed to catch on in the UK. At intervals someone re-discovers them and there is a little surge of interest and then all goes quiet. They are excellent from boats, and keep the bait out at right angles to the boat as it moves forwards. The planer is simply a flat piece of plastic set up so that it acts like a plug diving vane, but horizontally. So if the boat is towing it then it veers away from the boat and continues to do so. There is then no likelihood of it coming into tangling contact with a lure or bait trailed behind the craft, and a much greater extent of water is covered on one run. But once a fish takes it, it is rather an ugly way of fishing, with this great lump of brightly coloured plastic flap-

ping about. *Before* you get a take – it's good fun!

As you can see, modern boat fishing is very different from that pre-1960s. It is difficult to attribute advances, either in techniques or enthusiasm, to particular individuals, but Gordon Burton, following in the footsteps of Wagstaffe and Reynolds, must carry a lot of the blame! Dave Plummer and Jim Gibbinson were also successful but not so well known. More recently there have been splendid, thinking contributions from the likes of Dave Lumb, Dave Kelbrick, David Overy, even Neville Fickling, a reluctant lure fisherman who has led numbers of big-water safaris to Ireland. But we wonder if anyone has really surpassed the boat-fishing achievements of the Northern Irish Pike Society and The Pikers. They showed it could be done, in a way that surpassed the achievements of Wagstaffe and Reynolds, and thanks to their ambassador, George Higgins, we learnt of their progress and became inspired in Wales, England and Scotland.

A 31½lb fish taken on a trolled plug, 19 March 1975. Photo: George Higgins

Bob Templeton and George Higgins with a 21lb fish taken on a pikelet plug, 18 March 1989. Photo: George Higgins

27½lb to trolled perch, October 1977. Photo: George Higgins

A 26lb fish taken plug-fishing from a drifting boat, March 1984. Photo: George Higgins

ABOVE: *Playing a twenty-pounder on a small Irish Lake. Note that a hand-sized gaff was in use as late as the 1980s. Photo: Barrie Rickards*

RIGHT: *En route to the small lake, off Lough Arrow, seen in the previous photograph. Photo: Barrie Rickards*

A 29½lb pike taken on a trolled herring, June 1989. Photo: George Higgins.

Northern Irish Pike Anglers

George Higgins and his friends in the Northern Irish Pike Society and 'The Pikers' have been fanatical anglers on the scene of big-water Irish piking for many a year, as you can see from one of our photographs. Although most of us think of N.I.P.S. in association with George, it is a different grouping of seven anglers who comprised 'The Pikers' formed in 1974. N.I.P.S. was founded in 1976 and has had a varied membership over the years. 'The Pikers' club is one of the most successful in piking, now thirty-two years old, with its famous President, Packy Joe Reynolds, who sadly died in November 2004. The club still holds its friendly competitions on Lough Allen even though that water has declined: and six of the original seven members survive. Up to now they have caught 16,218 pike in 5,516 man days. Fish over 10lb number 3,798 and fish over 20lb 423. Twelve have been over 30lb, the best being Roy Smyth's two 36lb fish. Roy's total of twenty-pounders by August 2005 is 131 (not, as stated in Neville's list, 138). We are told that the youngest member, Alex Dickey, is in his forties and hence the only member contributing to the pensions of the rest of them!

The European Approach

It is not our intention to consider foreign piking in any depth in this book, but just recently a great deal of boating information is coming in from Holland, Sweden and elsewhere, which does suggest that we may have a little fundamental rethinking to do in the UK. Either that, or the Dutch waters are different, as some claim. Their approach to the use of jigs on big waters has certainly caught on, though more in the way of really new discoveries seems to apply to zander than to pike. Whatever the truth of this there is no doubt that further improvements in boat-fishing techniques will take place and one can hazard a guess that as far as big waters are concerned, some of those discoveries will come from Gordon Burton's experiences in North America.

9 HANDLING AND UNHOOKING PIKE

One of the greatest changes in pike angling concerns the landing, unhooking and general handling of pike, and it does no harm at all to remind ourselves of what went on for several hundred years before the developments of the last half century. In the first place pike were not netted. They were gaffed. As almost all pike were killed, this was perhaps no great matter. However, even this statement must be qualified. Pike were not so much killed as left to die, and this can take several hours. In the 1950s when almost all pike caught were not returned to the water, quite a few were eaten. Those anglers who took a fish for the table – and we have no objection ourselves to this at all – tended to kill the pike rather than simply let them expire slowly. But have you ever tried to kill a pike? It is extremely difficult, needing a very heavy blunt instrument at the very rear of the skull, or a big knife through the brain/skull. It's not like tapping a trout on the head.

Landing a Fish

As anglers took up the conservationist mantle and began to return their pike, again beginning in the 1950s, the gaff was still in use. It was soon realized that the round-bend gaff for salmon anglers was unsuitable for pike because all pike anglers needed was to slip the gaff point either under the tip of the jaw, or beneath the gill cover (not in the gills). When this was done the pike was usually slid to the bank rather than lifted out on the gaff. There was always a tendency for the active pike to swing itself on the curved gaff hook and leap free. So Richard Walker, an unlikely pike-friendly soul one might think, came up with the V-shaped gaff hook.

The Gaff
The V-shaped gaff was thoroughly tested in the 1950s by Barrie and found to be, as Ray Webb

A pike run. Pick up the rod, check the line, and strike.
Photo: Martin Gay

Not a sight we like to see, but less common these days: remains of a Lake District pike. Photo: Barrie Rickards

claimed, much better than the usual gaff. Small fish could be lifted out with very minimal damage, and larger fish could be slid to the bank with no damage at all. However, two things led to the demise of the gaff. One was an improvement in landing nets, happening at just that time. The second was the inefficiency of the gaff at the point just before the fish was gaffed. The angle of the fish had to be exactly right, and a hard-fighting fish never co-operated. Often you'd see the gaff flailing around ineffectively, damaging human as well as pike. Barrie was seriously unimpressed: if you've managed to get a bite, got the pike to the bank, the last thing you need is gross inefficiency at that stage. So for a year or two Barrie began to hand-land fish, but later devised and built a large round, folding landing-net frame. With a diameter of 30in (opened) it looked huge by the standards of the day. Prior to that he and Ray Webb used cycle rims (off sprint racing bikes) and 24in-round rims made by fitting two smaller, round landing nets together. He still has one made of stainless steel that was Ray's pride and joy.

Landing Nets

Carp anglers' nets were in use by some anglers and these were no real problem in that most anglers were fairly static and bait fishing, so a triangular frame was only mildly inefficient in its shape. The meshes were knotted, not micro-mesh, so there were no undue delays in unravelling the fish from the meshes prior to unhooking. Once landing nets reached decent dimensions they were soon seen to be much more reliable than gaffs, which were in serious decline long before a campaign outlawed them anyway. In uneducated circles, gaffs did persist for a few years, but the day of the gaff had gone by 1970.

There is a postscript to this story. The mobile lure angler probably kept the gaff going longer than the bait angler, because it is far easier to travel with one than it is to walk the banks with a landing net, especially a triangular one as we said earlier in the book (Chapter 4). Some anglers have still not resolved this matter for lure fishing but in the 1990s Colin Brett the Cambridgeshire piker came up with a gaff that had a smooth ball instead of a point. The idea was that it would not damage the pike at all, and would be easy to use. Both these turned out to be true but both Colin and Barrie found the same problems as before when it came to actually setting the gaff – so once again it was abandoned. Shakespeare was the company that made the prototypes for testing.

Unhooking

So in the late 1950s we had a situation where the landing net was creeping into use even though many sceptical pikers thought that pike would bite through the mesh! What happens then, when the pike is on the grass in the folds of the landing net? Well then, you used a gag to open its jaws. The gag is a variously powerful spring in different sizes for small and large pike, and it is squeezed in between the firmly clamped jaws of the pike before the pressure of the spring is released to force the jaws apart just prior to unhooking – so you can see the hooks in fact. If we tell you that only in 2005 did the tackle trade stop selling these tools it will give you some idea how long some improvements take to be widely accepted: Barrie abandoned the gag in 1957, almost half a century before the trade did. Clearly they had a use. If the pike is in nervous hands then perhaps a gag gives confidence. What it doesn't give is efficiency. In the first place it is very difficult to insert between the jaws. In all probability the teeth of the gag (rather like some V-shaped disgorges) don't do the pike any more harm than a big treble hook or two, but their inefficiency stems from the fact that the pike often throw them free – sometimes for yards – or they clamp down on them and don't open their jaws anyway!

Gags, Forceps and Gloves

Barrie used to lure-fish some small lakes at Eastrington in East Yorkshire, catching pike in the range 8oz–5lb as a rule. He used the smallest gag size, naturally, but the uselessness of the tool began to grate on him. One day he picked up a pike of around 3lb or so, putting one finger between the gill covers, under the lower jaw where they come together. To his surprise, the pike opened its mouth an inch or two. Then, by pushing the upper jaw with the other hand the mouth opened sufficiently to put the forceps in and

remove the lure. When the forceps went in the pike clamped shut again but soon opened up. Barrie never used a gag again. It seemed from then on a total waste of time to carry a gag.

So, from 1957 Barrie had a landing net, a pair of forceps and a spring balance. In the 1960s he and other members of the Cambridgeshire Pike Anglers demonstrated this technique both on the bank and at official demonstrations and lectures. It caught on quite quickly in the specialist-angling world but was adopted only slowly elsewhere and the gag survived for a few decades more. Even so, the gag, invented and used for a couple of hundred years, finally bowed out to the inventiveness of the modern angler.

We have mentioned forceps and need to say little more. They are a useful general tool for gripping and removing the hooks and today they are much tougher and come in varied sizes. Sometimes good long-nosed pliers are better and hook cutters (with long handles) are useful to have in

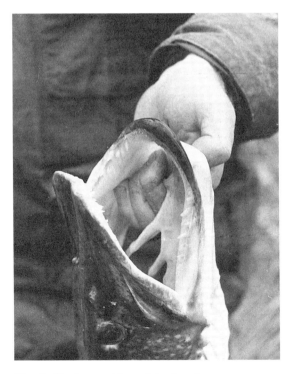

Handhold – better with a soft leather glove – preparatory to unhooking. Photo: Barrie Rickards

As the previous illustration, but with forceps in position. Photo: Barrie Rickards

LEFT: *After battling like this ...*

BELOW: *... and this the pike needs careful handling. Photos George Higgins*

an emergency. An improvement *was* made to Barrie's handling method, in that many adopted gloves to hold the pike, thereby lessening the chances of lacerations of the fingers by the pike's teeth. (Pike never attack you, unlike piranhas, but they do shake their heads from time to time.) If fishing properly a gloved hand and a good pair of forceps, pliers or hook-outs is really all that is necessary to unhook pike and this certainly accounts for 99 per cent of our unhooking.

Protecting the Fish – Lifting and Unhooking

Another improvement came in fairly quickly that eliminated lifting bigger pike off the ground.

For a right-handed angler the big pike is laid down on its *right* side, the angler's left hand, gloved or not, is put in the under-the-chin position, and then the pike's head is lifted slowly off the ground. The mouth opens or can be eased open in the usual way, and unhooking proceeds then as normal. When boat fishing it is not always necessary to bring the fish into the boat as it can be unhooked beside the gunwales, its body supported by water, the hand under its chin and the forceps doing their job. If you do lift a small pike off the ground then make sure the ground beneath it is soft, like grass.

A fairly early further improvement was the development of unhooking mats of soft foam.

These really do protect the fish and are probably better than grass. The fish is put down on the mat prior to unhooking and in some designs a fold of matting can be laid over the lower body of the pike thus preventing it thrashing around.

All the time these positive developments were taking place various disgorgers were being invented and used, from the simple V-disgorger, a large version of those used for unhooking cyprinids, to tools that embraced all three hooks simultaneously, to others with reversed Vs. The problem with all these is that they are designed on an incorrect premiss: that the pike will be too deep-hooked for the forceps to be usable. But the other big change in piking as described in Chapter 2, is that bite indicator systems and related procedures are now so good that deep hooking itself is becoming a thing of the past. By all means carry a disgorger if it makes you feel happier, but a pike hooked at the top of the throat, for example, is still far better unhooked by using forceps through the gill covers than it is by prodding around with a disgorger. In fact, a disgorger is rather difficult for one person to use and such procedures usually need two anglers.

What we are seeing in this chapter, and have seen in reality is the gradual abandonment of old, inefficient methods and their gradual replacement by techniques that are much better for the pike and save the angler a lot of fishing time in the process. We reckon most big pike on baits can be unhooked in less than thirty seconds, often much less. Lure-caught fish can take both a longer and a shorter time to unhook depending on the nature of the lure and its hook hold, but we are talking in seconds, not minutes in most instances.

Barbless Hooks

The matter of micromesh nets has been dealt with in Chapter 4 so we shall not repeat it here, except to say that it is not a good thing in piking. We have also discussed barbless hooks briefly elsewhere, but here we do need to expand a little. Barbless hooks came in to improve unhooking and became popular because they could be easily removed from micromesh nets. There is a downside to the seemingly admirable idea, and

that is that once anglers discovered just how *easy* it was to remove the hooks from pike they began leaving runs a little longer to increase the chances of hooking the pike further back than the jaws, in the soft tissue at the back of the mouth. This concept raised its head once before when back in the 1960s Ron Clay pointed out that this was the securest place to hook pike from the point of view of landing them. Anglers, however, turned against the notion because it is not in the best interests of the pike, and they should do so again.

Barbless hooks do not, in fact, increase the chances of the angler hooking and then landing the pike. Hooked at the front of the jaws there is a *much* greater chance of the fish coming adrift during the fight. Some very experienced anglers have argued the opposite but we believe they are landing pike because of their experience in playing of fish and not because of the inherently better method of hooking. True, a barbless hook will penetrate more easily: it will also un-penetrate more easily, and when a pike spirals, shakes its head or leaps, it can quickly come adrift. Just as a bait will fall off the hooks if so called semi-barbless hooks are not employed, so a lively pike will fall off. Indeed, on many of the pike we have landed on such rigs it is the hook with the barb on it that is doing the purchase, not the barbless ones.

Barrie first used barbless hooks in the late 1950s and early 1960s. It's an idea that at first sounds good – but isn't. There is a further problem with them that may not be confined to pike fishing. However, let's concentrate on the pike. If a fish is hooked towards the top of the throat, with barbless hooks, then the heart may be penetrated – that's where the heart is and in pike it is far from fully protected unlike in some species. Barbless hooks penetrate deeply, far more deeply than barbed hooks, which usually only go in just above the barb, and they can penetrate repeatedly during playing. Barbed hooks penetrate once, and stay that way as a rule. In soft flesh, which we try to avoid, both barbed and unbarbed penetrate similarly, but barbless can go in and out.

Martin Gay landing a large pike. Photo: Martin Gay

We would go so far with barbless-hook protagonists, but no further: we accept that on many hooks the barbs are still much too large. In the 1950s Barrie created his barbless hooks by pressing down rank barbs or filing them down. He realized after a while that only the tiniest of barbs was needed to do the job well – what later became known as microbarbs. It is likely that microbarbs are all that is needed in almost all fishing, being very efficient and with no drawbacks. So on this subject we feel that many innovative modern pikers are heading in the wrong direction albeit with the right motives for the most part. And in lure fishing, barbless hooks have no place at all, whereas microbarbs on hooks might be the best answer of all.

In short, therefore, get rid of micromesh nets in piking, use microbarbs or pressed-barb hooks, and we've got things about right. None of this is about our own convenience: it's about the convenience of pike.

Handling the Pike

We have now reached the point in this chapter where you may well feel we've been a bit long-winded, but these are important debates. Anyway, now we have the pike on the grass, the unhooking mat, or the bubble plastic, and it is unhooked. What next? Well, here is another area

that has from time to time been the subject of heated debate. Of course, if it's a small pike one pops it back quickly into the water. An easy way to do this is to carry it in the unhooking mat and slide it in. Or one can lift it under the jaw, as you might during unhooking. If the latter method is used it is important that the fish is not dropped, which is possible if it suddenly flips. A glove does help here, giving a better grip and with experience one soon learns when to lower a fish to the ground if it starts to leap.

How Long Out of Water?

The problem is not really with small fish but with large ones. Do you really need a photograph? How should you hold the fish for a picture? How long should this take? We really are going to be blunt now: far too many big pike are out of the water for far too long whilst numerous pictures are taken or even video films. This lengthy handling is unnecessarily long, is thought by many to be causing a decline of big-pike fisheries, sometimes in as little as two years after the big fish were 'discovered': this subject was discussed at some length at the 2005 Pike Angler's Club Convention in Leeds, and members of that organization pledged to investigate the matter. Trout fisheries with pike fishing seem especially at risk and it does seem that the fast-growing fish in such waters are more fragile than slower-growing pike elsewhere.

This matter does need thinking about. We have fished waters where the pike were just as fast growing as in trout fisheries (that is, 20lb fish were only five years' old) but the fishing did not decline until a major salt pollution killed them off. The superlative fishing lasted ten years and showed little, if any, signs of change. We know other waters, including one that Barrie has fished for thirty years, where 20lb fish are about seven- to eight-years' old, and here too, no signs at all of a decline in productivity. These waters have one thing in common: they are fished by relatively few but very experienced pike anglers. Could it be that the magnetic attraction of trout-water pike brings in too high a proportion of anglers inexperienced in handling big fish? Let's face it, very few anglers are experienced at handling pike over 30lb, and it is fish of this weight that seem most at risk in the sense that it is just these fish that first 'disappear' from a new water. Malcolm just recently caught a pike a few ounces short of 30lb. He was fishing on a rocky and steep dam wall. With the help of a friend, he unhooked the pike while still in the water. Safely inside the landing

Barrie Rickards landing a pike. Photo: Barrie Rickards

net, three quick photos on an unhooking mat at the water's edge and the pike was returned. Just a few minutes' work. The pike, which had not been re-caught for over eighteen months, was again re-caught by Malcolm's friend just ten days later. So *we* must be doing something right.

Poor Handling

We have, ourselves, witnessed poor handling of big pike on trout waters. On one occasion a 30lb-plus fish was not returned to the water for fifteen minutes. In that time it had been videoed, and at least a full 36-frame 35mm film run off on it, all with the fish held in different poses. Five minutes of that time was spent in unhooking the fish, which is four and a half minutes too long. Big pike are actually much easier to unhook than small pike. If there is any problem at all with unhooking then the fish should be placed in a keepsack until everything is ready – tools or the right people, or whatever it takes. Exactly the same approach should be made with respect to photographs. Get everything ready first, and then take the fish out of the water. A big pike should not be out of the water for five minutes – two to three minutes is all that is necessary. Do you *need* thirty-six photographs? Video it by all means as long as the cameraman is nothing to do with the landing, unhooking and weighing of the fish. And don't wait for the cameraman: it is his job to fit in with you and the fish, not vice versa. Our feeling is that trout-reservoir pike are not intrinsically more fragile than other pike but that they are, by the nature of the intense fishing, subject to unnecessary bad handling. It has been claimed several times in the press that some so-called experienced anglers are as much to blame as beginners, but we have seen no real evidence of this. We cannot think of *any* experienced pikers who keep the fish out of the water too long, but we do know of some who do not strike as quickly as we do. Some have them on the bank longer than we do ourselves, but, even so, we are talking only two to three minutes.

Weighing

A moment or two ago we mentioned the weighing of pike. How should one go about this? Again the modern pike anglers have improved matters greatly. Even in the 1970s most of us simply hooked the spring balance under the chin and lifted. It was quick, but had the disadvantage that any wriggle from the pike could dump it on the ground. Some anglers used to put the pike in a net, even the landing net, which is a safer way but slightly inaccurate. Others used a wet polythene or other sheet, which was altogether kinder on the pike. Then Eddie Turner came up with a weighing sack of smooth material, weight – 10oz when wet. Malcolm has the large size – 12oz when dry, and big enough to hold most big pike. It was a logical and sensible idea, and Barrie and Malcolm still use an original bag from Eddie's stable, 'ET Tackle'. When the fish is returned to the water, it can be carried there in the weigh sack and simply slid into the swim.

Keepnets and Keepsacks

Perhaps we should again dive back in time to make a contrast with what the modern piker does. Nowadays most pike are returned immediately

A lean Autumn fish being handled carefully before return. Photo: Martin Gay

after capture, although some may be retained in a keepsack for weighing or photography, usually for a short time (and never overnight, when oxygen levels may fall, resulting in death of the fish). In the past some numbers would be kept in keepnets, and of the old, knotted variety too. There were two reasons for his: one was to avoid spooking any other pike in the swim; the other was to get a 'bag' photograph. It is now known that returned pike do not spook other pike in the vicinity; and 'bag' pictures have declined because they take too long to execute, thus putting the pike at risk. Although it is irrelevant to the modern scene it is, nevertheless, worth noting that those odd old keepnets did not damage pike if the nets were properly staked out and covered over. They were not, however, as good as modern keepsacks. Keepsacks are a godsend and can be used on most, though not all, waters. For example, they are to be discouraged where there is a strong water flow, a big tidal range, or the banks are excessively steep, as well as in Fen drains where the water level may change drastically in half an hour. In general, however, they are extremely useful.

Photographing a Pike

How should one hold a pike for a photograph? This is under debate as we write and has been so in the past. Historically pike were laid on the grass or held horizontally with the belly sagging between the captor's hands. The inexperienced angler holding a pike can often be identified by the fact that he wraps one arm around it! I suppose we ought to mention, although we are slightly reluctant to do so, the fact that at the beginning of the last century many pike were held up by their eye sockets. If the pike were dead then it becomes only a matter of aesthetics, but if alive then it is seriously anti-conservation in outlook. This practice continued much longer in Ireland and was still widespread in the 1960s. Pennel in 1865 argued against this hold, which simply shows how long a good idea can take to really be accepted. Dead pike appeared in all manner of poses, mostly unsatisfactory (on pig-scales, hanging down a wall, suspended by string, and so on), not least because they were dead and looked like what they were, creatures that had once been alive and were now on their way to degeneration and decay. A picture of a freshly caught pike, alive and in good condition, which in a few seconds will be swimming free, is quite a different and much more satisfactory story. In most circumstances it's better than a stuffed pike, even though the latter may give pleasure and cause awe, long after the allotted life of the fish itself. Malcolm has recently had all his photo scrapbooks bound up in leather and gold lettering. They look superb and the cost, just £200.

Another method of holding fish, and one you will often see, is where the angler grips the pike firmly at the back of the head, a technique often used also when handling bream (although not carp we notice). Bill Chillingsworth used to hold his fish in this manner, and we have tried it out ourselves. It is not as secure a method as we describe below, and is unsatisfactory altogether for fish over 10lb because considerable pressure is then needed. It would be best if we abandoned this one.

Unhooking Technique

In the 1960s, as anglers began to learn the new unhooking technique, which we described at the beginning of the chapter, they also began to take pictures of the fish held in that position, either held up off the ground, or with the head and part of the body off the ground. Of course, the traditional horizontal pose was, and is, used as well. Most anglers learn quickly that if you hold the pike in a particular way it is possible to avoid the sagging belly shot! The head-up shots avoid this anyway, as do pictures of the fish lying in the grass or the mat.

However, the question raised by some anglers is this: does the head-up shot or the sagging belly shot put undue stress on the internal organs of the fish or on the body structure of the fish? We recall this being discussed back in the 1980s by Shaun Greaves, an angler who seems to have disappeared from the scene these days. Whilst it is a good idea to think about this and discuss it, it does seem to us a little far fetched. For example, pike leap clear of the water naturally, without the

help of anglers, and at such times must put the body to 'stress' in the air, not to mention the impact of hitting the water again. Air is no more difficult a medium for fish than water is for humans: and both can spend some time in the 'alien' environment without problems. There is a further test: on those private waters where only we fish, there has never been the slightest indication of damaged or lost fish. It's all a question of how quickly, smoothly and skilfully the handling is done. That said, we would recommend that when holding a fish aloft, with one hand beneath its chin, the other hand should be used to support it. The bigger the fish the less inclined we are to do this, and the more inclined we are to the horizontal pose or the fish-on-the ground shot. Some anglers will go to great lengths to get the 'impact' photograph, perhaps because they need to illustrate a column, and this also is an area that does need thinking about. For example, if you catch a fish while you are afloat and you cannot get a good picture, is it fair on the fish to head for shore? This takes time – the boat has to be beached, tied up, and the fish transferred to shore. We've seen this happen and it has the beginnings of unscrupulous behaviour in it.

Put the convenience and health of the fish first, that is the modern motto, at least if you want to preserve your piking.

An Example of Good Handling

We can give a good example here, although it would be far from the only one in our own experiences. When Barrie caught his best pike to date, a thirty-five-and-a-half-pounder a few years ago, he found himself in a bit of a quandary. On his own, the nearest human being, if anyone was at home, was about a mile away, perhaps a little more than that. The water in question was not one where you could ever use a keepsack, for several reasons. Although he had a self-shot system he didn't have it with him on the day: it had been left at home along with anything else that added to the weight on a long walk. So he simply laid the fish on the grass, on his landing net, and took several quick pictures for his record. The fish had been unhooked, weighed, measured, photographed, and returned inside three minutes, so far as he could tell. Malcolm once returned a new PB pike (over 31lb) without a photo. He then embarked on a campaign to re-catch the same pike. Many trips later he caught a 33lb 4oz pike, this time taking a photograph.

Playing the Fish

There is one final aspect of fish handling that we haven't dealt with, and that is, what happens before the pike actually hits the landing net? In other words whilst the fish is being played. Far too many anglers take far too long to play pike. Look at it like this: you cannot break a 15lb BS line by putting a serious semicircular bend in your rod. All you are doing here is putting on a pressure of 3–4lb at most. So *bend* the rod whilst you are playing a fish. Too many anglers, after an initial hard strike or firm pull, allow the pike to do all the work and the rod top merely tap taps away, hardly bending at all (carp anglers also do this, frequently). This prolongs the fight too much and the pike will be more fatigued on landing than it need be. Give the fish some welly, get it in to the bank and get it netted. The unhooking and handling techniques we have outlined in this chapter are perfectly capable of handling a lively pike on the bank.

If you operate quickly, a lively pike on the bank translates to a lively pike returned to the water.

Summer Piking or Winter Piking

Related to this is the whole question of summer piking versus winter piking. Quite a number of serious pikers, such as Des Taylor, have doubts about the risks posed by summer piking, the principles of which are outlined in the previous paragraph. Get the fish back quickly. The actual tackle is crucial in summer, if less so in winter. We would not contemplate fishing with lines under 15lb BS (monofil) and in many circumstances would be using braid with breaking strains of 30–60lb depending on the water and the expected size of pike. The metabolism of pike is raised in summer and, after spawning in March or April, they are still lean rather than fat, so they travel much faster, leap much more, spiral beneath the

surface, and generally are more of a handful. Be prepared both mentally and physically and operate quickly. We do not ourselves consider summer piking 'a bad thing', preferring to do it correctly, and to educate others to do the same. The debate has arisen because a new generation of summer pikers is with us now, and some may well be inexperienced in this aspect of the sport. However, over decades, education of pike anglers has succeeded so well, it does seem a retrograde step to give up on it now.

The Approach to the Successful and Proper Handling of Pike

- When playing pike, bully it to the bank as quickly as possible.
- Use a capacious landing net, preferably round in shape and with a non-micromesh netting material.
- Bag the fish to the bottom of the net before lifting the net out.
- To lift out the net, grasp the rims of the net frame and lift vertically or *gently* slide the capture up the bank.
- Lower the net to the grass, an unhooking mat, or bubble plastic.
- Hold the fish down briefly, using both hands if it shows a tendency to flex (this precedes flapping around).
- Part the netting, free any hooks from the netting.
- You should be using microbarb, pressed barb or small barb, small hooks.
- Use the hand unhooking technique outlined in the beginning of the chapter. Take the hooks and rod away from the fish.
- Slide the pike into a weighing sack and weigh, using a pre-corrected balance to weight fish up to 32lb or even 40lb.
- Hold for a picture, over the unhooking mat or grass.
- Lower into weighsack and return to the water as soon as possible.

---

10 DISTANCE FISHING

Very little distance fishing was done in the remote past and only a small amount in the first half of the last century. Even that was more the working of a bait than getting real distance. One could argue that the best way to fish at distance on any water is to use a boat. That was not an option on many waters, so what did anglers do to get around the fact that a 100yd cast is unusual if one has the full clutter of bait, lead and float?

Pike on a drifter rig. The photo was taken with the camera in the left hand and the rod in the right hand, by Barrie Rickards.

Alternatives to Using a Boat

Floats and Feathers

We think it was Spence (Table 1) who first used a feather on top of the float. This actually works quite well, and we have used swan feathers or, rather, parts of them. However, you cannot move the bait a great distance, but it does help to move it and work it a bit. If there's a good back wind, which you are able to catch, then a good stiff feather *will* get you well out on the lake, but it's not a reliable method. There is one thing about it that is correct, and that is the use of a more or less two-dimensional sail, as on a sailing boat, with a little curve.

After feathers, angling designers took a backward step, the authors included, going for vanes with three blades at 120 degrees. You could also work a bait with these but they were no better, possibly worse, than feathers; Barrie now knows this from wind-tunnel experiments. (On an entirely different subject, a three-vaned dart *turns* the object to which it is attached, giving it a little stability in its medium, air or water, but it cannot be used to catch wind and propel the bait.)

Plastic Vanes

Then came further attempts to improve on the feather. Several famous anglers, including John Sidley and Colin Dyson, made plastic vanes that attached to the top of a cylindrical float. Catch the wind and they worked. Furthermore, it was possible to cast them well, enabling the angler to cast beyond the calm water round the margins and increase the chances of catching the wind. We have used these drifters to effect up to 200yd and it does not matter a deal that the drift is slow – it's covering water. There is, of course, a depth problem. If the float is fixed or sliding then the water must be deeper than the setting, otherwise it will not drift. There is an exception here: that is, when using a big drifter, sprat or small livebait as bait, and a light lead, and you are fishing over a clean gravel-pit bottom, the bait can be made to drag the bottom, or fish just above it, trailing a light lead, and the big drifter does the work. This can be deadly.

Everybody had just got used to using these Dyson Drifters when the inimitable Eddie Turner, then running Eddie Turner Tackle, (E.T.), came up with the E.T. Drifter. We spoke to Eddie at the T.A.C. conference in Leeds recently. It was sad to see the E.T. Tackle range on display and the one and only Eddie Turner not employed on that stand. Not our business of course, but we feel someone is missing a trick here. This man always thinks outside the box and he has now produced a drifter rig that has yet to be surpassed. It consists of a *large* rectangular, plastic sail set on a thin, long, wire stem. The 'float' is one or more black polyballs that stabilize the outfit just below the surface film. The long stem projects still deeper

and is attached by a swivel to the line. It is devastatingly effective and huge distances can be reached quickly. It still has the same problem with relation to depth, as does the Dyson Drifter.

There are ways of getting around the depth problem. Suppose, for example, you have 50yd of 6ft-deep shallows to cross before you hit water 12ft deep. What you can do is tie up the drifter with PVA so that it is at, say 4ft, or to the end of the trace swivel, and have a stop knot at 10ft. In ordinary winter weather the PVA will last until the float crosses the shallows – and if it does not, then you simply tie a bigger knot.

Ballooning

Ballooning is a less popular but very effective way of fishing and has the advantage that the basic rig solves the depth problem immediately. A paper clip is attached to the top swivel on the trace and is then push-fitted on to the knot of the balloon. It needs to be so set that a good pull will release the balloon. The stop knot is positioned in the usual way. It is not as easy to catch the wind as it is with a drifter rig, in that you cannot cast the balloon at all, but it catches the wind better than any drifter and really travels out across the water at high speed. Quite often you have to hold it back, and it is a sobering moment when, occasionally, you are unable to strike off the balloon. It simply emphasizes how difficult it must be to reach the bait on the strike, effectively, at, say 250yd. Ballooning enables you to use the bait on or off bottom, which is a definite advantage.

Of course, a released balloon goes careering across the countryside, but hardly constitutes litter and probably gives someone else a little pleasure. On one occasion, Barrie and Martin Gay were ballooning baits out to the middle of an Essex reservoir. Off came the balloons, and they bobbled across the water, one of them finally finishing up against some reed beds on the far bank. Not long afterwards a posse of twitchers arrived, armed with space telescopes, and began observing (one assumed) some birds in the reeds. Suddenly, one of the balloons exploded, sounding just like one of those bird-scarers. And it did. All the birds left the reed bed in a mighty hurry and the birdies' prey was gone. And there was no evidence remaining as to the cause of the explosion. Martin and Barrie, in great innocence, sat on their seats on the opposite bank several hundred yards away. Barrie surreptitiously took out his binoculars. Martin remained doubled up on his chair. Only someone who witnessed Martin Gay laughing helplessly can know what this was like.

Radio-Controlled Boats

The final development in distance fishing was the design of radio-controlled boats to do the job of carrying out the bait (and groundbait too if needed). Barrie is not experienced in this field though did spend some enjoyable days with Jim Housden on a Suffolk reservoir they were fishing at the time. Jim had an early but quite workable boat, which would take out deadbaits easily. It wasn't so easy getting livebaits out there, but this may have changed recently. A second (safety) rod was always used because in those days one could not guarantee that the craft would return! Sometimes, the wind was difficult and at these times it seems power was lacking. Jim's boat went out with a line attached that had no tackle on it, and once the bait tackle had been pulled into place he wound back the boat on the spare rod. Some of the boats we have seen in modern times are quite magnificent. Malcolm has owned a microcat baitboat for two years, (cost £1,000). He has caught a good number of 20lb-plus pike at distances up to 200yd and in September 2005 he took two pike in two hours at long range weighing 29lb 10oz and 21½lb. He also used the bait boat to good effect on a new water, again taking a 29lb and 24lb pike on the same day. He recently wrote an extensive article, 'Baitboat Piking' for *Pike and Predators* magazine, emphasizing the need to strike a run very quickly whether using 15lb mono or braid as your line. At such distances, you need a 3oz minimum lead to anchor your bait. It seems old dogs are still learning new tricks.

This leads us now to the question we have deliberately avoided so far, namely, is distance

necessary? Well, yes, but not in most circumstances. Most of the waters we fish, especially rivers, drains and canals, can easily be covered by ordinary casting. It is worth, now, pointing out the differences between the past and the present. In the 1950s, up until the mid-1960s, it was not possible to cast big deadbaits very far with conventional rods. Most of the rods in use were soft in action, such as the Mk IV carp rod. You simply could not cast a big herring on a Mk IV. so you threw it out by hand, or used a long, forked stick (leaving the reel pick-up in the open position, and the rod in good rod rests). Sometimes, the line caught in the nick cut in the tip of the throwing stick and the herring hit the lake surface in a kind of reverse Polaris launch. On other occasions, the pick-up was left on, or the rod rest snagged the line, and the rod itself attempted launch velocity. In the end Ray Webb had a very large aluminium casting spoon made at the steel works where he was a telephonist. This was attached to a very firm casting rod, and he could then chuck deadbaits around 40yd or so, occasionally accompanied by something extraneous, such as half a reed bed.

Glass Rods

When the new hollow glass rods came along, such as the Davenport and Fordham 'Farstrike', the Sportex carp/pike rods and the Oliver's stepped up carp rods, chucking a large deadbait became easy. We still use these rods occasionally and they are fine. We use them when electric cables are in the vicinity, as these and carbon fibre go together rather too well for comfort. When the value of half baits was recognized (Chapter 2) unheard of distances were achieved. Barrie had – indeed still has – a homemade fibre-tube blank with which he could cast half baits (*with a float rig*) to the opposite bank of the Relief Channel, a distance of 100yd. An interesting discovery was made on the subject of slow-taper, soft rods (which all the above were, being designed on the Mk IV principle) versus fast-taper rods. The latter were in vogue down in Kent and Essex in the 1970s, and were used to fire sprats a long way, coupled with a big casting lead of up to 3oz. Using an Olivers rod, Barrie consistently outcast Martin Gay who had been brought up on fast-taper rods. When Martin used the Olivers rod as a trial he quickly outcast Barrie, but a 100yd was sensible top whack in real fishing.

Some anglers in those days could never see the sense of fishing in, say, the middle of the Relief Channel at around 60yd. They argued that the pike would be along the edges, by the reed beds. Richard Walker argued the same. They were wrong. Barrie took twenty-pounder after twenty-pounder, fishing at range, whereas those who fished the margins had very few pike, let alone big pike. Ray Webb also suffered here, because he couldn't use his inadequate tackle to cast. So he used Barrie's on occasions – and caught twenty-pounders.

As a general rule pike are where they are, not where we think they should be. Sometimes, they will be in the margins, at other times not. Hotspots are not restricted to the marginal areas, and in the Norfolk Broads, both Bill Giles and Edwin Vincent recognized this (*see* Giles' chapter at the end of Fred Buller's book, *Pike*), so there is a good case for being flexible and for having the ability to cover as much water as necessary. On occasions, balloons, drifter rigs, bait boats and distance casting will be necessary, and we have the wherewithal to do it. It is exactly the same argument we used in Chapter 3 on the holistic approach to piking. Those who are versatile physically and mentally will succeed. Those who choose to hamper themselves will succeed less well. Malcolm's results with a bait boat prove this.

Alex Dickey with a 28lb fish from a big water. Photo: George Higgins

11 THE NEW MILLENNIUM

The second half of the last century was, we have argued, one of enormous change in pike angling to the extent that it comprised a revolution, nothing less, in techniques, and understanding pike, pike ecology and the philosophies surround pike fishing. We have tried to identify the roots of that revolution during the late 1950s and early 1960s, showing how the innovators, although they stood on the shoulders of giants, actually introduced a deal of new thinking that overturned almost all that had gone before in bait fishing. The lure-fishing revolution, for such it was too, followed later, overshadowed by the advances in bait fishing in the 1960s. It began in the 1980s and is still with us today.

The new piking came about because some individuals thought 'out of the box', especially Bill Giles, Fred Taylor, Ray Webb, John Neville, Tag Barnes, Dave Steuart, Ron Clay and the colleagues with whom they fished. Not long after them came a host of anglers who quickly set about improving the new 'basics'; to name a few: Martin Gay, John Watson, Jim Gibbinson, Neville Fickling, Colin Goodge, Mick Brown, Rian Tingay, Terry Eustace, Bill Palmer, Jim Housden and Eddie Turner. There was, obviously, some overlap with the earlier innovators, all the latter continuing to contribute to change; and there were others we haven't mentioned because we do not know a deal about them.

George Higgins with a 16¼lb fish, Loughin island, a trout-water pike on a pikelet plug. Photo: George Higgins

A New Era

These revolutionaries or visionaries, call them what you will, were followed in the 1980s and 1990s by the new breed of piker we describe in Chapter 7. There is, however, a thread in all this that we have not yet discussed, and which may well be blossoming in the 2000s, namely, the tendency to seek out big-pike-yielding waters and to fish them until the angler gets his prize. This may or may not be increasing the pool of knowledge in the pike-fishing world. Most certainly it is a subject under hot debate as we write this book so it will be of interest to see how it pans out in the long run and whether it benefits anglers or not. Some of the criticism one hears of the big-fish hunters is simply jealousy and comes from people not prepared, or unable, to put in the time, effort and money to succeed with giant pike. We need to be more dispassionate in our analysis than that. It is important to consider the question properly for two reasons, at least; one is that real revolution, in any sphere, is often followed by a period of mediocrity where band-wagoners do nothing to advance the 'cause'; a second is that there may be a risk of unsavoury activity, which would reflect badly on pike angling, currently on a popular wave, and on angling in general therefore.

Nige Williams

What we'd like to do now is paraphrase Nige Williams from his new book, *Just Williams* (2005). Nige is the most successful of pike anglers when it comes to pike of 30lb, having caught more than anyone else. Come to think about it, since he caught his first twenty-pounder as a youngster in 1981 he is probably the most successful pike angler anyway, if you take the trouble to work it out. We haven't! If you read *Just Williams*, and we strongly recommend that you do, then have a careful read of pages 67–69 entitled 'Strategic Pike Fishing'. You will read the thoughts of a very, very focused man. Where the water is does not matter. Who and how many are fishing the water doesn't matter. He has a rough plan for the season, involving a few waters that have yielded 30lb

pike or near 30lb pike; but he is prepared to modify this at a moment's notice if he hears of a big pike either through the press or the grapevine. He'll go to some trouble to locate the water and swim, even though details of the water may not have been released. As he rightly says, most things leak out these days, especially after a little persistent questioning. We are now in the Internet and text message era. Malcolm, fishing on a Pennine reservoir, heard his friend talking to another piker fishing on Windermere.

You will notice that nowhere in this section does he talk about looking for a water he can enjoy fishing; or searching out completely new waters; or worrying about odd rules and regulations that might impinge on his enjoyment. All these things would be important to your present authors, but Nige is much more focused on catching 30lb fish than we are. When Ray Webb and Barrie wrote *Fishing for Big Pike* in 1971, they said that twenty-pounders were a reasonable target for most pikers, but that you couldn't target 30lb fish, not least because there were so few waters that had any. Well, now you can. We have mentioned Nige Williams because he is the most successful at doing this, but there are others around today doing the same thing and achieving catches that to most of us are staggering. They may not be quite so single minded as Nige, but their efforts are impressive nonetheless.

It is important that we state our position on this one. We are far from opposed to anglers who take this approach. On the contrary, it seems perfectly valid to us, and each person should fish how and when he likes, given the assumption that his methods do not adversely affect pike or the sport of other pikers. We have heard criticisms of this modern approach in that it is thought by some not to advance the understanding of pike or the techniques of their capture. This cannot be correct, because the first thing you notice about those anglers – and this is abundantly clear in *Just Williams* for example – is that tackle and techniques are not only honed to efficiency (which we extolled in Chapter 3) but that the angler is simply bursting with ideas. Talk to Nige Williams for five minutes and you'll see what we mean. You don't have to catch 30lb pike to be able to advance piking for everybody; but if you *are* doing so, then you certainly can advance piking. Again, and just to emphasize this point, read Nige William on boats.

Nige has been criticized so he tells us, for 'failing' to catch 30lb pike from really big waters. So he answers this by giving the average of Blithfield, Derravaragh, Ladybower, Bough Beech and Belvide (average is 570 acres!). He does point out, however, that some even bigger waters, Mask, Beg and Lomond *are* more difficult, and on these waters it really might be difficult to target 30lb fish.

Back to the 1950s
It is interesting now to go back a bit in time and have a look at how things used to be and to see if we can pinpoint how this focused approach has arisen. It's probably incorrect to say that it has always been there as an approach. In the 1950s most pike anglers fished their local waters and were happy enough to improve their catches on a season-by-season basis. A few anglers made pilgrimages, to Ireland, to the Broads, to Slapton Ley (a now forgotten water) in Devon, or even to Bosherton, made famous by Clive Gammon. With the establishment of specimen hunting in the 1960s, anglers did begin to move further afield and to seek out new waters. Journeys of one to two hours there and back became commonplace for most of us, and of course more people had transport of their own to do this. Even so, most anglers still wanted a nice day's piking, in pleasant surroundings, accompanied by a few friends. The crack was as important as

Alan Ritchie, with a 23¼lb pike on trolled roach, and George Higgins. Photo: George Higgins

the piking, and you see this in all the writing of the time, or in the autobiographies, which record that time: *Fishing for Big Pike* sold as well as it did partly because of the anecdotes it contained. Indeed, from communications in recent times, Barrie is aware that anglers remember the stories and pay less attention to the 'instructional' sections.

There were, however, a few anglers in those early days of modern times who *did* target big fish and waters where a big fish was known to have been caught. Ray Webb was the first one that Barrie came across and he was focused in exactly the same way as Nige Williams. He went, quite literally, all over the UK, chasing up reported big-fish captures. Barrie did not have the time or funding to go with him, except when the search was nearer to home, such as in Fenland. There was once a report of a good 20lb fish from 'a small drain' in the Fens. The next weekend saw Ray, with Barrie in tow, interviewing dozens of people, mostly non-anglers, and by the end of the weekend they had not only located the captor, a young lad in his teens, but the water and the actual swim from which the pike was caught … and, naturally, all the details of bait and tackle. They found out where to get a permit and later on Sunday afternoon negotiated with a farmer so that they could arrive within 100yd of the swim itself, rather than walk three-quarters of a mile. (The youngster had cycled.) That little drain did see some attention from anglers from the boy's village for a few weekends, but after that Ray and Barrie had it to themselves and caught a fair number of different twenty-pounders, over several seasons, up to 24lb.

This was the way Ray Webb worked and it was exactly the same principle as that adopted by Nige Williams. In the case just quoted, it resulted in fishing that was acceptable to Barrie, in that it was reasonably remote, quiet and had no rules to worry about. And the fishing was good. The water was never going to produce a 30lb fish and never has, the best being 25lb, but they learnt so much when fishing it that it stood them in good stead in the future. Even so, it can be argued that they owed it all to the helpful young man.

1950–2006

From that time to the present day there have always been some seriously focused anglers. Perhaps they are a little bit less concerned with the surroundings and company than they are with the results. Each to his own choice really, given the provisos we mentioned earlier. Martin Gay and Barrie were once taken to a (then) secret lake, which was thought to hold some very big pike. Neither of them was interested in pursuing the matter because fishing conditions were abysmal. It simply was not their scene. They decided there and then that they'd stick to twenty-pounders in Essex and the Fens. Not long afterwards, the then not-so-secret water produced a number of thirty-pounders – in the most abysmal circumstances. So we have this kind of angler too, to whom aesthetics in angling *do* matter.

2006

To date, we have really only mentioned Nige Williams, but others are also setting the pike-angling world alight with their spectacular captures. We do not want to suggest that any of them are so totally engrossed that they do not want friends or a nice water to fish, and nor do we suggest that of Nige Williams. But these are all well focused, and are very successful pikers. Most of them give slide shows for other anglers, some write books, others articles in the press; perhaps they are no different to those old lads, all those years ago, in the 1960s, who made *their* mark at the time.

Dave Horton

Let's take Dave Horton. The summary of himself that he gives in his book, *Ultimate Pike* (2000), is revealing to a degree. This is the first pike book of the new millennium and it sets the tone we feel, confirming the way things seem to be going: 'A year later I caught my first twenty and so began an obsession that has forced a whole series of change on my life'. He changed career from engineering to the fire service so that he could work shift patterns to fit in with his piking. He isn't the first of our heroes to do that. Ray Webb also gave up a job in an engineering factory and took a shift job as a telephonist with the Post Office, just like John Neville. The shift work allowed them to get in a lot of fishing. It is not professional fishing, but it is as close as you can get. Dave's obsession 'contributed in no small way to the failure of my marriage'. This is where most anglers draw the line, putting family before fishing, and only the obsessed do otherwise. Talk to Dave Horton and you soon realize that he is much more than the compulsive big-pike angler that he portrays. He just enjoys piking. Between 1985 and 2000 – a mere fifteen years – he'd caught well over one hundred twenty-pounders, including eleven over 30lb. That is some progress from the time he started, perhaps comparable to the achievements of Nige Williams. One difference is that Nige puts fishing second to his home life, even though when actually fishing he really does work it out.

In total, Dave has taken 182 pike over 20lb, including fourteen 30lb fish (fifty-three over 25lb). One interesting feature is that on thirty-nine occasions he has taken two or more twenty-pounders in one day, with three in that category in one day on three occasions. Given that all this began only in 1984 it is somewhat impressive, particularly as twenty-eight different waters are involved. Dave, with his angling side-kick Vince Duberry, did especially well at Abberton Reservoir (where Martin Gay cut his big-pike teeth). In the winter of 1988/9 he and Vince had twenty-three twenty-pounders and their remote controlled boat, one of the earliest, produced over half of the big fish. Dave continued his run of success with big pike from a small lake, from Ardleigh Reservoir and in Ireland and Scotland as well as the Fens. As do so many of our great anglers, Dave has contributed to magazines such as *Coarse Fisherman*, *Pike and Predators* and, particularly, *Pikelines*.

Phil Wakeford

This also applies to another of the new millennium stars, namely Phil Wakeford. If you read Phil's chapter on gravel-pit piking in Dave Horton's book, you realize just how much work you have to put in to succeed. We were reminded of Mick Brown's similar efforts in Lincolnshire gravel pits or, earlier, Martin Gay's results (also to 30lb plus) on the Essex gravel pits. Phil also draws attention to the fact, of which only a few are aware from personal experience, that very big pike in gravel pits can remain uncaught for a very long time to the extent that they are often thought to have died. Malcolm has also found this on the large Pennine reservoirs. Some of the very large pike show once a year or even up to eighteen months between recaptures. Possibly this is something only realized fully in recent times. We know of a 5-acre pit, which regularly produced a small number of quite well-known big fish, to 24lb and yet, having been fished very regularly with baits everywhere, suddenly produced a pike of 32lb, which had never been seen before, and was never seen again.

Phil also exhibits exactly the same degree of focus as Nige Williams and Dave Horton, and if you read his section in the above-mentioned book entitled 'Developing a plan' you'll see what we mean. Most anglers don't develop a plan anyway, but just take pot luck from weekend to weekend. There is, however, one rather sad but quite unarguable note in Phil's writing when he says, at the end of that section, '… When a particular pit is on song it does pay you to make that extra effort to fish it fairly hard as it certainly will not last more than a season or two…'. This really does seem to be a message for this millennium. Too heavy a fishing pressure ruins a water in a couple of seasons, and it doesn't have to be a trout water for this to happen. One can address this matter personally if one fishes a private or secluded water and one keeps quiet about catches, but too often crowds of anglers move in and the fishing is ruined. For some, such as ourselves, the fishing is ruined before that moment because we do not enjoy competing in crowds. The behaviour of crowds of pikers often leaves a lot to be desired. If they all behaved quietly and performed well with the pike's interest at heart, then it wouldn't matter, but a lot of them don't. Phil Wakeford has recently accepted the President's position at the P.A.C.

Derek MacDonald

Another angler with almost incomparable results is Derek MacDonald. He is reported in *Angling Times* of December 2005 as having caught eighteen thirty-pounders of which no fewer than five have been over 35lb. All this in just a few short years' fishing. We have had just over this weight in a very long time of fishing, which puts his catching achievements in perspective. Derek now owes us all a book, we think, telling us how he goes about it. We suspect that the word 'focus' will be involved somewhere.

Steve Rodwell

Steve Rodwell is a most successful Fenland angler with well over one hundred twenty-pounders to his credit. One of the things that interests Barrie about Steve's approach is that he sets a much greater store by features than Barrie does. Features such as drain widening, joining ditches and so on do produce fish, but it seems to Barrie that drain hotspots are not related to these features as a general rule. He readily accepts he may be wrong. Other than that, Steve's approach to fishing Fenland waters seems very close to our own. We particularly like his attitude to the leap-frogging technique so well liked by small groups of anglers. 'Slow it down,' says Steve, and he is right. We would add: 'do it quietly'. Big pike take time and because you are so close to them on a small drain, it is crucial to tread softly. Most of the keen pikers we have watched on Fenland drains do tread softly, and not only that, but keep a low profile. When there is a good high bank it is easier to merge in with that if not too colourfully dressed and one moves slowly, but where banks are low it pays to keep well back from the water's edge.

One of the great features of Dave Horton's book, *Ultimate Pike*, is that it brings together not only ultimate pike by anyone's standards, but many of the best of the new-millennium anglers. We have mentioned some both in this chapter and elsewhere. Others include James Gardner, Nick Peat, Phil Pearson and Andy Walker. It also includes an overlap with some of the 'oldies'. We can remember Mick Hopwood's forty-pounder and the staggering catches made by Jim Housden too. In Chapter 3 of this book we reported how in the 1970s and 1980s anglers were vastly more efficient than at any time previously, and the results to this new breed of anglers (Chapter 7) showed it. Given all that efficiency and skill, what is it that makes the anglers of the new millennium just that bit more successful? If it can be encapsulated by one word we think Nige Williams got it when he talked about focus. Those anglers concentrate very seriously on catching big pike. All their planning is towards finding the waters with the giant pike in them, and then working out the timing and techniques to succeed. They have probably now taken this approach just about as far as it can be taken. Or are we prejudging them even now?

Great Piking Books

It has been an astonishing story running now for fifty years, and who are we to say it is at its zenith. It may be, but perhaps 40lb fish will become as common in the future as 30lb fish are today. Common is not quite the right word, of course. As we put the finishing words to this book, we hear of a 41½lb pike caught by Alan McFadyen. He also had had three other pike over 25lb. These came from a 'private' Scottish trout water that had not been discovered, and obviously had received very little angling pressure. How long that will last remains to be seen. We'll end this chapter by showing how this marvellous progress is echoed in the very book titles through the half century.

Geoffrey Bucknall wrote his book *Big Pike* in 1965 and when he did so he intended to convey where we were then and how impressive big pike had been caught. When Ray Webb and Barrie wrote *Fishing for Big Pike* in 1971, they tried to explain advanced methods and a route towards big pike. Then Eddie Turner wrote *Mega Pike* in 1990, showing that giant pike could be a realistic target. Finally, we have Dave Horton with *Ultimate Pike* in 2000 and throughout much of this period there has always been Fred Buller's classic, *Mammoth Pike*. Whatever next? *Alien Pike* perhaps!

EPILOGUE

We have tried to write this history without making it an instructional book as such, concentrating rather on the great anglers and how they took it to where we are now, to a level of piking never before seen. There is instruction involved, naturally, but perhaps more important is the thinking behind it all. So have we now reached the stage, implied in the last chapter, where methods and approaches are so sophisticated – and efficient – that there is nowhere else to go? Probably not. As we implied towards the end of the last chapter there may yet be unthought-of revelations (Barrie is working on a totally new concept at present, for example!).

Where Next?

However, there is another way of looking at all this. Half a century is less than the lifetime of many of us who are still piking successfully. Those of us of a certain age, and who have contributed to piking all our lives, give or take a few years, went through a number of stages not unlike those gone through by the sport as a whole. Thus we began with a questioning mind; we came up with a variety of solutions; we became very efficient; and we became very focused ourselves and successful *for the time*. (Others then followed, and achieved more, not only in catches, but also in understanding.) The point is, we are still alive and kicking, most of us. We are still catching pike, occasionally good ones. What we do, though, is put to the forefront of our fishing the companions we fish with, the places we fish and the methods we choose to use. There are signs that many anglers, after their initial 'successful' period, turn to this philosophy. Neville Fickling, for a long

time one of the most single-minded pikers, if not the most original-minded, has recently stated that who he fishes with and where he chooses to fish are increasingly important to him. All this may seem obvious to some because different people enjoy things in a different way. If you read Jim Housden's chapter in *Ultimate Pike* you will see that he too reached a similar conclusion with respect to that superlative chalkpit from where quite a few of his giant pike came. In the end he became a little bored. As we know Jim well we know that he loves his angling company, special waters and problems: in short, a challenge or two. There were signs, even in the 1990s, that some anglers were beginning to prefer an easier, comfortable approach to piking, and this is to some extent reflected in Malcolm's (1993) book, the title of which gives away the emphasis being sought: *Tales from a Pike Angler's Diary*.

It may be that we shall go this way in a collective sense. More anglers may fish purely for 'enjoyment' rather than for 'results'; we have placed those words in inverted commas because without them it suggests an extreme position that probably never obtains with anyone. There *could* be a new movement. To some extent we already see this happening. Pike-angling bodies are the Pike Anglers' Club of Great Britain, the Lure Anglers' Society and the Pike Fly Fishers' Association. You only have to read their magazines to realize that many anglers just enjoy piking, as well as the social component that goes with it in a society: the P.A.C. piking convention for example; or the L.A.S. and P.F.F.A. gatherings at the waterside. As we write this the P.A.C. 'Old Farts' section is about to be formed! This is to be a social element of P.A.C., membership open to old stagers who will meet at dinners, perhaps with a few honoured guests, and tell piking stories until the small hours, and maybe have a drink. Perhaps from time to time the thoughts of those veritable sages might be sought on piking problems!

Fly Fishing

We have not discussed fly fishing for pike in this book very much because it is a relatively new thing. There have always been a few pikers using flies, but now they have formed a club. Whilst improved fly-fishing techniques have certainly stemmed from the club members, especially the advocation of suitably powerful rods (nine or ten weight) and appropriate lines, most of the activities are social, such as the annual (very) friendly match on the River Delph in the Fens. There has been some criticism of *summer* fly fishing for pike, but if suitable gear is used and the fish given some welly, then it can be no more problematical than summer lure fishing. Both have to be done properly, of that there is no doubt, and we are sure these matters will continue to be discussed until pike fishermen are satisfied with the outcome in terms of pike welfare. Fly fishing for pike in winter is certainly a good option and Barrie's best fly-caught pike of 20½lb came from a Fen drain in winter. There's little weed and less of a backcast problem for a start! So pike fly fishing is a new boy on the block, but it's here to stay.

The Pike Anglers' Club

Let's turn our attention now to the P.A.C., its past achievements and its future role in pike fishing. We could also mention other pike clubs too, but as past officers of P.A.C. we have a better idea of its overall functioning. The first attempt at a national pike society (The Pike Society) in the early 1970s was not a success. The time was right for one, and the demand was there, but organizationally it failed to function. Its first President was Fred Buller, followed by Barrie, although we are not blaming either of them for the poor showing of the body. After pressure from Eric Hodgson, himself no mean piker, Hugh Reynolds and Barrie, of the Cambridgeshire Pike Anglers, agreed to try again, this time with the P.A.C., but entirely on their terms. Both were very busy in their careers and

they decided that the normal democratic system would not fit in with the other demands on their time. They opted for a benign dictatorship system, to run for about three years, then to be replaced by the same. They made all the decisions and got on with it. It worked well, and still does, because officers do not stay too long in the post, bringing great drive and initiative, and then hand over to a new team of 'volunteers'. Such a system may not last forever but it has served well to date.

P.A.C. has always sought to improve the lot of the pike and of the pike angler. In many areas they have succeeded. Most certainly the kill-all-pike attitude has gone and the unnecessary killing of pike is becoming much rarer. P.A.C. has never argued against taking the occasional fish to eat, even though most members would not do this, but such acts hardly affect the overall ecosystem in which the pike is a major player. The lot of the pike has improved in others ways, too: we have tried to explain in this book just how pike-friendly is tackle today and the manner in which it is employed. Similarly pike angling itself has greatly improved, with quality fishing in many areas even though there are far more pike anglers around.

The early P.A.C. days were heady times. Everybody was working extremely hard. We have already mentioned Ron Pendelton (who attributes his apprenticeship in piking to Brian Culley and friends) but other names we do not hear quite so much of now, but who were vital, include Phil Tew, Graham Stead, John Tate and John Roocroft.

Setting Standards

These people set the club standards, enthusing and helping newcomers into the sport, and helping them in proper fashion so that they knew how to fish. They spread a good message far and wide. Some people who came on board P.A.C. were already members of established specimen groups such as John Roocroft and the Three Counties Specimen Group. They had terrific catches over the years and put the Shropshire Meres region on the map. By 1984 they had already caught over 500 double-figure pike, with fifty twenty-pounders from that region. So active catching was taking place even in the early days of P.A.C.

In this book we have painted generally a rosy picture of the sport of pike angling. Almost gone are the days when pike were unnecessarily slaughtered. Tackle, techniques and piking philosophy have also improved dramatically in the last fifty years to the extent that a real revolution has taken place. The number and variety of waters available to pikers has increased and, without any doubt the quality of pike angling – and hence the basic ecosystem – has for the most part improved. As we write there has never been a time before when it is easier to catch a big pike from a wide range of geographical regions in the UK.

Some Concerns to be Addressed

But for all this, there is a note of worry, an undercurrent of concern, which bothers numbers of seasoned and experienced pikers. The number of pikers has increased and in two ways: firstly the actual numbers of pikers has increased; secondly, individual pikers fish more often nowadays than they used to – often every weekend for months at a time. Prior to our revolution the average piker might have half a dozen trips in a winter, if that. More rods per angler per day are used now, up to four in fact. In the old days it was unheard of to see more than one pike rod in action, and that was usually as a second string to a bottom rod. This was the norm in the 1950s, and before. Ray Webb and Barrie felt very strange at first, using two rods in the early 1960s, and fishing only for pike on a day's outing.

Another factor is that there is probably a big turnover in pike anglers today. That is, a youngster takes it up, gives it a few years, and gives it his all at the time, then drops it for something else like young ladies or beer. But they often came back to the sport in later life. Because there is now no apprenticeship in angling as a whole, let alone pike angling, it is easy to start piking in the fast lane and, later, to crash there. Anglers coming into the sport like this need a fast learning curve of training and if they fall within the orbit of P.A.C. and its members, or a similar club, then all might be well. But the majority do not: and nobody knows just how many such anglers there are and what the turnover rate is.

Everything in the last two paragraphs adds to the pressure on pike stocks and if things proceed further in this direction only the most careful and vigorous and extensive education will help, for we cannot expect new pike waters to grow on trees. We shall not easily be able to mop up the increasing number of newcomers and train them well. The angling magazines have always helped enormously, of course, but the worst kind of angler doesn't read anything. There is another matter too, and one that seriously concerns some of our correspondents who have contributed to this book. Quite a number of anglers whom we respect greatly for their contributions to piking have complained that in some quarters, amongst pike anglers of sufficient experience that they should know better, those in 'the numbers game' put the pike at risk. That last phrase is the one most widely used by some of our writers: that some anglers are so concerned with building up a list of big fish to their name that they are not careful enough with their pike handling.

We have to say that this last worry is very difficult indeed to identify, let alone quantify. We ourselves have seen on many occasions pikers taking far too long to unhook and return their catch. This often involved extensive photography sessions. It is partly to address the worries here that we wrote in detail in Chapter 9 on the handling of pike, and advised, for example, on the best ways of dealing with photography. But what our correspondents are telling us is that the offenders *know* what they should do, but simply don't bother – in the interests of backing up their capture with loads of pictures, and maybe they leave the runs too long as well, using barbless hooks, hooking the pike relatively deeply, and so on.

It is quite difficult to know what to do about the cowboys in our ranks. We feel that there are not too many in this particular category and that most of the bad handling is done by the inexperienced, not the experienced. But perhaps a culture change is now necessary.

Malcolm's own club has quite recently taken a long lease on a large (190 acres) Pennine reservoir. Water levels fluctuate in the summer and winter. As these are drinking water reservoirs, at all times the banks are stony. The standard of pike angling by some was very poor, hence Malcolm has insisted on a set of pike-preserving rules.

Better Pike Fishing

Anyone who has not got the correct pike-fishing tackle is asked to leave the water. We think that the P.A.C. should press the N.F.A. very strongly to ensure that all member clubs should enforce these rules. Southport A.A. are showing the way forward. Only then will we stop the cowboys. It will also ensure any newcomers, young or older, know what is expected of them when they go pike fishing. Modern pike angling has its roots in the specimen-hunting movement, and at the core of that movement is the philosophy that one *can* get results if one applies oneself to it. So results themselves become a measure of success or otherwise – not necessarily of *enjoyment,* but of success. Again, we have a little sympathy with this viewpoint, after all, in the 1950s there were many articles written by pike anglers who clearly did not catch many pike, and in reality were far from experienced. For this reason alone, Ray Webb and Barrie gave some publicity to their catches and the results, experience, call it what you will, form the basis of *Fishing for Big Pike.* However, the numbers game can be carried too far: it does not mean, for example, that an angler listed at the bottom of

George Higgins being George. Photo: George Higgins

Neville Fickling's list is not as good a pike angler as the one listed at the top! Results in themselves are a really crude measure of success. In any case, success really means, 'Do you enjoy your piking?' Some of those involved in the numbers game clearly did not, for despite big catches they gave up fishing after a few short years. For others like us it's a long and enjoyable lifetime: your two authors have now clocked up eighty years of pike fishing between them. That's some experience.

It is obvious that continuing education of pikers is very necessary, of young and old, inexperienced or not. The P.A.C. must investigate fully how it is that 'overfishing' on a 'named' water leads to its demise as a top-class water in three years or so. Is it all down to bad handling of pike? If so, are there *other* aspects of bad handling that we have not touched upon in this book? We were brought up short by an article in 2005 by Neville Fickling who pointed out that at the legendary Blithfield very few big pike were repeat captures. He asked the questions: 'Do all the caught big pike die, or do they avoid anglers in future?' The second question does seem unlikely, and yet we recall Arthur Russell's tiny water where a 32lb fish turned up once only, having never been seen on lesser weights, and was never seen again. Possibly the truth is somewhere between the two.

All these questions will need to be examined by pike anglers in the next decade. In addition, it might be a good idea if pikers were encouraged more, by articles and by example, to extol other features of the sport than the numbers of big fish caught. There is little more boring at a lecture than to see fish pose after fish pose for an hour, whether the fish are big or not. Many of us keep a diary of both facts and events, but the lists in those diaries are of little more than local interest unless half a century has passed. Maybe our hopes are rather pie in the sky, and yet, it is beginning to appear, a slow change *is* taking place. Pikers *do* now seem more interested in the how, why, where and who than in just the catch itself. So there is hope, surely? We have better pike fishing than ever in our history. We have better tackle and know-how than ever before. Perhaps before too long we'll have a better idea of why we do it.

BIBLIOGRAPHY

Pike Fishing Books (COURTESY OF THE P. A. C. AND MALCOLM BANNISTER)

Bailey, J. & Page, M., *Pike: The Predator Becomes the Prey* (The Crowood Press, 1985)

Bannister, M., *Tales from a Pike Angler's Diary* (Sandholme Publishing, 1993)

Batten, D., *An Introduction to Pike Fishing* (The Crowood Press, 1989)

Bickerdyke, J., *Angling for Pike* (Upcott Gill, 1888)

Brown, M., *Pike – The Practice and the Passion* (The Crowood Press, 1993)

Bucknall, G., *Big Pike* (Angling Times Book, 1965)

Buller, F., *Pike* (MacDonald & Co., 1971)

Buller, F., *The Doomsday Book of Mammoth Pike* (Stanley Paul, 1979)

Buller, F., *Pike and the Pike Angler* (Stanley Paul, 1981)

Buller, F., *Tactics for Big Pike* (Beekay Publishers, 1985)

Buller, F., *Great Pike Stories* (Medlar Press, 2003)

Buller, F., *More Mammoth Pike* (Medlar Press, 2005)

Cholmondeley-Pennell, H., *The Book of the Pike* (Robert Hardwicke, 1865)

Cholmondeley-Pennell, H., *Pike and other Coarse Fish* (The Badminton Library, 1885)

Church, B. (ed.), *Big Pike* (The Crowood Press, 2006)

Fickling, N., *Pike Fishing in the 80s* (Beekay Publishers, 1982)

Fickling, N., *Pike Fishing with Neville Fickling* (published by the author, 1992)

Fickling, N., *Everything you need to know about ... Pike Fishing* (published by the author, 2004)

Fickling, N., *Mammoth Pike* (Lucebaits Publishing, 2004)

Gay, M., *Beginner's Guide to Pike Fishing* (Pelham Press, 1975)

Gay, M. & Rickards, B., *Pike* (The Boydell Press, 1989)

Gibbinson, J., *Pike* (The Osprey Anglers Series, 1974)

Gray, T., *Pike Fishing: Red Letter Days and Others* (Heath Canton Ltd, 1923)

Gustafson, P., *How to Catch Bigger Pike* (Collins Willow, 1997)

Hampton, J., *Hampton on Pike Fishing* (W and R Chambers Ltd, 1947)

Harper, S., *Broadland Pike: A History of the Largest Recorded Captures* (published by the author, 1998)

Holgate, J., *Big Water Pike Fishing – Book One: Bank Fishing* (Cast Publications, 1989)

Holgate, J., *Big Water Pike Fishing – Book Two: Boat Fishing* (Cast Publications, 1990)

Horton, D. (ed.), *Ultimate Pike* (published by the author, 2000)

Jardine, A., *Pike and Perch* (Lawrence and Bullen, 1896)

Lumb, D., *Modern Pike Rigs* (Cast Publications, 1992)

Marlow, J., *The Pike Fisherman's Handbook* (Stanley Paul, 1966)

Martin, J.W., *Days Among Pike and Perch* (J.W. Martin and Co., 1907)

Miles, T., *Pike Fishing* (The Crowood Press, 1991)

Moules, D., *The Fenland Thirties — A History of Fenland Pike* (published by the author, 2003)

Page, M. & Bellars, V., *Pike: In Pursuit of Esox Lucius* (The Crowood Press, 1990)

Palmer, W., *From Dimples to Wrinkles* (published by the author, 1997)

Pennell, C., *The Book of the Pike* (Robert Hardwicke, 1865)

Phillips, D., *Pike* (Beekay Publishers, 1990)

Pike Angler's Club of GB (ed.), *Basic Pike Fishing* (P.A.C., 1986)

Pike Angler's Club of GB (ed.), *Advanced Pike Fishing* (P.A.C., 1987)

Pike Angler's Club of GB (ed.), *Pike Fishing Beyond 2000* (P.A.C., 2000)

Pullen, G., *Go Fishing For Pike* (Oxford Illustrated Press, 1990)

Pye, D., *The Way I Fish* (Angling Times, 1964)

Rickards, B., *Pike Fishing Step by Step* (Cassell, 1976)

Rickards, B., *Big Pike* (A & C Black, 1986)

Rickards, B., *Success with Pike* (David & Charles, 1992)

Rickards, B. & Bannister, M., *The Ten Greatest Pike Anglers* (Boydell, 1991)

Rickards, B. & Gay, M., *The Pike Angler's Manual* (A & C Black, 1987)

Rickards, B. (ed.), *The Best of Pikelines* (Boydell, 1988)

Senior, W., *Pike and Perch* (Longmans, Green and Co., 1900)

Sidley, J., *River Piking* (Boydell, 1987)

Spence, E., *The Pike Fisher* (A & C Black, 1928)

Turner, E., *Mega Pike* (Beekay, 1990)

Venables, B., *Fishing for Pike with Mr. Cherry and Jim* (Angling Times, 1961)

Ward, A.L., *Pike (How To Catch Them)* (Herbert Jenkins, 196?)

Watson, J., Master Fisherman: Pike (Ward Lock, 1989)

Watson, J., *A Piker's Progress* (Creel Publications, 1991)

Weatherall, N., *Pike Fishing* (Witherby Library, 1961)

Webb, R. & Rickards, B., *Fishing for Big Pike* (A & C Black, 1971)

Whieldon, T., *Pike Fishing* (Ward Lock, 1987)

Whitehead, K., *Ken Whitehead's Pike Fishing* (David & Charles, 1987)

Willett, R., *Let's Start River Pike Fishing* (The Crowood Press, 1990)

Williams, N., *Just Williams* (Lucebaits Publishing, 2005)

Wilson, J., *Catch Pike with John Wilson* (Boxtree, 1991)

Winship, W. (ed.), *Pike Waters* (Boydell, 1990)

Lure and Fly Fishing Books

Barder, R., *Spinning for Pike* (Arco Publications, 1970)

Bettell, C., *The Art of Lure Fishing* (The Crowood Press, 1994)

Hanna, A., *Fly Fishing for Big Pike* (Coch-y-Bonddu Books, 1998)

Harris, C. & Harris, S., *Encyclopedia of Lures* (The Crowood Press, 1993)

Holgate, J., *Catching Pike on Lures* (Castabout Publications, 1991)

Holgate, J. (ed.) *Lure Fishing for Pike Volume 1.* (Castabout Publications, 1987)

Holgate, J. (ed.) *Lure Fishing for Pike Volume 2* (Castabout Publications, 1988)

Ladle, M. & Casey, H., *Lure Fishing – A New Approach* (A & C Black, 1988)

Lumb, D., *Pike Fishing with Lures* (published by the author, 1996)

Pritchard, M., *Spinning* (Collins, 1984)

Rickards, B. & Whitehead, K., *Plugs and Plug Fishing* (A & C Black, 1976)

Rickards, B. & Whitehead, K., *Spinners, Spoons and Wobbled Baits* (A & C Black, 1977)

Rickards, B. & Whitehead, K., *Spinning and Plug Fishing* (Boydell Press, 1987)

Scott, S. (Jock), *Spinning up to Date: Trout, Salmon & Pike* (Routledge, 1932)

Spencer, S.S., *Pike on the Plug* (Witherby, 1936)

Thurlow-Craig, C., *Spinner's Delight* (Hutchinson Library, 1951)

Thurlow-Craig, C., *Baitmaker's Delight* (Hutchinson Library, 1953)

Veale, S., *Fishing Lures: A Practical Guide* (Sportsman Press, 1992)

Other Titles of Interest to the Pike Angler

Berners, S., *A Treatyse of Fysshynge wyth an Angle* (1496)

Buller, F., *Book of Rigs and Tackles* (Paulton House Publishers, 1967)

Fickling, N., *In Pursuit of Predatory Fish* (Beekay Publishers, 1986)

Gray, T.S., *Pike Fishing* (Heath Cranton, 1923)

Harper, S., *Angling Afloat: A Complete Guide for Coarse Fishermen* (The Crowood Press, 1989)

Hill, N., *A Fisherman's Recollections* (Herbert Jenkins, 1944)

Morgan, P., *The Pike Angler's Library: A Guide to British Pike Fishing Books* (Coch-y-Bonddu Books, 1998)

Nobbes, R., *The Compleat Troller* (T. James for the Helder, 1682)

Powell & Owen W., *The Rudiments of Angling* (B.H. Matthews, The Cabot Press, 1912)

Pullen, G., *Go Fishing for Pike* (Oxford Press, 1990)

Turrell, Dr W.J., *Pike Fishing* (Seeley Service & Co, 1953)

Walton, I., *The Compleat Angler* (First Published in 1653)

Zeiske, W., *Esox: The Story of a Pike* (English edition) (Richard Sadler Ltd, 1970)

AUTHOR BIOGRAPHIES

Malcolm Bannister

Malcolm Bannister was born in Southport, Lancashire, in 1946. Little did he realize as a young boy that his early experiences, catching sticklebacks in the small clearwater ditches on the wetlands joining the River Ribble estuary, would one day result in him spending thirty years in search of the freshwater shark known as the pike, *Esox lucius.*

He started fishing for pike on 21 June 1976 when he caught his first ever pike on a Mepps spinner. He estimated the fat 30in pike at 9lb. He joined the old Pike Society and was also present at a meeting held in September 1977 in Bourne, Lincolnshire, which resulted in the formation of 'The Pike Anglers' Club'. In the summer of 1977, with the late Barrie Burton, he began to use livebaits and quickly learned the dangers of keeping pike out of the water for too long in hot weather. The pike fishing season did not start until October in many parts of the country. During those brief summer months Malcolm caught over one hundred pike from his local Crossens Drain. He had served his piking apprenticeship.

In 1985, just nine years later, he was the Secretary of the P.A.C., having put together a very strong team of Southport and Lancaster-based pike anglers who ran the club for three years and for which they were made Honorary Life Members. He had a strong interest in lure fishing and in April 1992 he wrote to Doug Stange, editor-in-chief of the famous American *In Fisherman* magazine. Doug sent Malcolm what he had asked for – two videos previously unseen in this country. Malcolm had them both converted to the European PAL system and in August of 1992 his reviews on American-style jerk-bait fishing, and a fly fishing for pike video, were published in *Pikelines Magazine* no 57. Such was the response that Malcolm (Treasurer & Membership Secretary) along with Dave Lumb (Secretary), Barrie Rickards (President) and Geoff Latham (Chairman) made the decision to form 'The Lure Angler's Society'. His timing was again spot-on for the lure revolution has been spectacular to say the least. In June 1992 he also had imported into this country what must have been the first batch of the famous 7in Suick Lures courtesy of Frank Suick. The following summer in a catch of over 150lb he took two doubles to over 15lb on a Suick at the June 1993 LAS Esthwaite Water fish-in. Two weeks later whilst filming once again at Esthwaite water he caught a pike of 23lb 12oz – one of the first 'Video' twenty pound lure-caught pike in this country. He was once again with Barrie Rickards filming in Barrie's classic film *Success with the Lure*. At the 1994 Esthwaite event he caught pike of 21lb 4oz and 30lb 6oz and a week later he caught a 22lb pike on a 7in Suick – the first Suick UK-caught twenty perhaps. He also arranged for Harris Angling to market the Suick Lures.

After three years at the helm Malcolm and the committee handed over to a new team, which included the old 'gent', Derek Gibson and a young Dave Kelbrick. The outgoing committee of the LAS where made Honorary Life Member's for their services to the society.

Malcolm has during his thirty years as a pike angler written many articles for various magazines and he co-authored with Barrie Rickards *The Ten Greatest Pike Anglers* in 1991 (The Boydell Press). This book is the definitive history of pike angling up to the early 1950s. He also had published his own pike-fishing story in *Tales from a Pike Anglers' Diary* by Sandholme Publishing in 1993. He wrote on Lake District pike fishing in *Pike Waters* by Bill Winship (The Boydell Press, 1990).

Malcolm has caught twenty-pound plus pike from waters as varied as Loch Lomond to the Fenland Drains. He has fished most of the Lake District waters successfully for many years. During the past five years he has concentrated his efforts on the bleak but picturesque Pennine moorland reservoirs. His largest pike of 33lb 4oz (2 December 2001) came from such a water just 45-minutes drive from his home. Just recently he caught two pike of 29lb 10oz and 21lb 8oz in two hours from one such water. He has caught four pike over 30lb in weight, all appropriately from his own native county of Lancashire – before the 1976 boundary changes. He considers himself a piking all-rounder having caught 30lb pike on livebait, deadbait and lures. Most of his pike fishing is now done with deadbaits during the winter months.

He regards his local Crossens Drain pike of 22lb (December 1999) as one of his most memorable captures, as pike of that weight on that water are very scarce indeed. He also takes an active interest in his local angling association, having been Secretary of Southport & District AA for almost 25 years. He lives with his wife Victoria and their cocker spaniels Little Dan and Jet, with which he likes going for long walks on the Pennine tracks high above the waters he loves to fish. He plays the violin rather badly (so he's told) and collects early campaign medals when funds permit.

Barrie Rickards

Barrie Rickards retired recently from the University of Cambridge, Department of Earth Sciences at the age of 67. He is now Emeritus Professor of Palaeontology and Biostratigraphy at the University and will continue research there into the evolution of fossil groups and at the same time increase his consultancy role for geological surveys, oil companies and so on. Barrie is a Life Fellow of Emmanuel College, Cambridge. He might do a bit more fishing!

Barrie grew up in Leeds and Goole in Yorkshire and fished the East and West Ridings of Yorkshire as a boy: the Rivers Ouse and Derwent as well as many clay and borrow pits. He has been a club official every single year since 1955, in offices as varied as Senior Treasurer of the Cambridge University Angling Club to Fishery Manager for Waterbeach Angling Club. Currently he is a Founding Fellow of P.A.C. (past Secretary of P.A.C.; past President of the Pike Society); President of the Lure Angler's Society and Pike Fly Fisher's Association, as well as being President of the Specialist Angler's Association (S.A.A.) (past President of N.A.S.G. and N.A.S.A.). He has represented anglers over many years on various consultative committees associated with the Environment Agency or its predecessors, and recently chaired the E.A. investigation into water resources in north-west Norfolk (The North West Norfolk Catchment Abstraction Management Strategy; March 2005; www.environment-agency.gov.uk/cams).

He has published well over 700 articles in magazines from several countries as well as the UK; and this is his twenty-sixth fishing book. He has published one novel with angling overtones *Fishers on the Green Roads* (Medlar Press) about youngsters growing up in Yorkshire just after the Second World War. He has contributed numerous chapters to fishing books. Currently he is completing *Walker: Biography of an Angling Legend*. With Malcolm he wrote *The Ten Greatest Pike Anglers*, a historical study taking us up to the 1950s. Although Barrie specialized to some extent in pike fishing this was a direct consequence of his summers being taken up with student examinations, student field trips and his own fieldwork. The tench remains his favourite quarry and he hopes to catch his first 10lb fish in 2006. He has taken nearly 2000 10lb+ pike, well over 200 over 20lb, and six over 30lb, his best being 35½lb. Other good fish include brown trout to 16lb, barbel to 12½lb, roach and rudd to 2lb 14oz, Nile perch to 120lb, sea trout to 7lb, rainbow trout to 7½lb, and skate to 30lb. He has yet to catch a 30lb carp, which is another (minor) ambition. His best bream was 8lb 6oz, and dace 14oz. He hopes that like Bill Giles he'll still be fishing when he is 92.

INDEX